Essential
Florence and
Tuscany

by
ROBERT KANE

Robert Kane is an art historian specialising in
Renaissance poetry, art and architecture. He has
written several guides to Italy.

GW00337520

AA

Produced by AA Publishing

Written by Robert Kane
Peace and Quiet section
by Paul Sterry
Original photography
by Barrie Smith

Edited, designed and produced by
AA Publishing.
© The Automobile Association 1994.
Maps © The Automobile Association
1994.

Distributed in the United Kingdom
by AA Publishing, Norfolk House,
Priestley Road, Basingstoke,
Hampshire, RG24 9NY.

A CIP catalogue record for this book
is available from the British Library.

ISBN 0 7495 0869 8

The Automobile Association retains
the copyright in the original edition
© 1992 and in all subsequent
editions, reprints and amendments
to editions listed above.

All rights reserved. No part of this
publication may be reproduced,
stored in a retrieval system, or
transmitted in any form or by any
means – electronic, photocopying,
recording or otherwise – unless the
written permission of the publishers
has been obtained beforehand. This
book may not be sold, resold, hired
out or otherwise disposed of by way
of trade in any form of binding or
cover other than that in which it is
published, without the prior consent
of the publisher.

First published January 1992
Revised second edition May 1994
Reprinted November 1994

The contents of this publication are
believed correct at the time of
printing. Nevertheless, the
publishers cannot be held
responsible for any errors or
omissions or for changes in the
details given in this guide or for the
consequences of any reliance on the
information provided by the same.
Assessments of attractions, hotels,
restaurants and so forth are based
upon the author's own experience
and, therefore, descriptions given in
this guide necessarily contain an
element of subjective opinion which
may not reflect the publisher's
opinion or dictate a reader's own
experience on another occasion.
**We have tried to ensure accuracy
in this guide, but things do change
and we would be grateful if
readers would advise us of any
inaccuracies they may encounter.**

Published by AA Publishing, a
trading name of Automobile
Association Developments Limited,
whose registered office is Norfolk
House, Priestley Road, Basingstoke,
Hampshire, RG24 9NY.
Registered number 1878835.

Colour separation: Mullis Morgan
Ltd., London

Printed by: Printers Trento, S.R.L.,
Italy

Front cover picture: Duomo

Maps and Plans

This book employs a simple
rating system to help choose
which places to visit:

✓	'top ten'
◆◆◆	do not miss
◆◆	see if you can
◆	worth seeing if you have time

INTRODUCTION

The 'flowering' city is how Firenze (Florence) may be translated – and its coat of arms is the lily. Its beauty, and the beautiful things its people have created over the ages, are the reasons why visitors from all over the world come to Florence: the city of the lily clustered around the bud of the great dome of its cathedral is a landmark of Western culture, set in a fair and smiling countryside rich in food, wine and sunshine.

Florence is famous above all for its Renaissance art – for the paintings of Botticelli and the sculpture of Michelangelo, the genius of Leonardo and the thousand contributions of a host of other artists and master craftsmen of greater or lesser renown. In the 14th, 15th and

A flower of a city, Florence blossomed during the Renaissance

16th centuries Florence was truly a hothouse of art, a magnet attracting artists from all over the rest of Italy and a 'school' that could still teach even when its pupils began to go abroad to find patronage. One of the world's greatest painters, Raphael, came from Urbino and went on to Rome, but Raphael would not have been Raphael without his Florentine education. However, Florence was first and foremost a city of literature – the city of Dante – and even before that the city of merchants and bankers – the city of the Medici – and it was only on this platform that its pre-eminence in the visual arts was built. Florence has the great virtue of being a small city – though sometimes, when the summer crowds are greatest, that may not seem such a virtue. Finding your way about and getting around are easy, even though there are plenty of alleys and backstreets. Fortunately the authorities have finally curtailed the amount of traffic permitted to circulate through the centre. The centre is compact and can be walked around easily – quite unlike those of Milan, Naples, Rome or Venice or most other European cities. The population of 650,000 is modest by today's standards, and Florence has not greatly expanded since its heyday in the Middle Ages and the Renaissance.

Of course some changes have taken place over the ages, and there is plenty of industry (notably round the nearby town of Prato). However, both the capital and the numerous hill-towns of Tuscany have retained their character – a special combination of ruggedness and elegance unparalleled elsewhere, even in Italy. Tourism may be the main economy of Florence, but a second wonderful characteristic is that, despite the heritage of Michelangelo and the enormous wealth of its historic art, Florence is a city very much alive. Florentines have lost nothing of their famous wit, their acute business sense, their accurate connoisseurship and their discriminating taste for food, wine and fashion. There could not be a greater contrast with Venice, which is truly a 'museum' city: Florence pulses with its own life, tourists or no tourists. All Florentines bask at least a little in the glory of Dante and Michelangelo, and believe in their hearts that they know better than others how to live. It is easy to be convinced that they do – they know both how to work and how to play, both how to be practical and how to be elegant. Do not be deceived by their sharpness – for while Florentines have no patience for fools, they are genial and generous in many other ways. A visit to Florence is an indispensable part of everyone's education – not simply for the wealth of its art, which has been preserved through the centuries thanks to the city's keen and early awareness of its heritage. However many times you return there is always more to discover, in one of the most dense and fascinating square miles anywhere. This treasure is also surrounded by some of the most entrancing countryside in the world, and by a host of smaller towns, each of them worth a trip.

The Ponte Vecchio carries shops and the ducal escape corridor across the Arno

BACKGROUND

The heyday of Florence stretched from the 13th century to the 16th. Though there was a town where Florence is in Roman times, it was not prominent, and it was only in the changed conditions of the later Middle Ages that geography and other factors favoured the rise of this city that 'revived' the glory of old Rome more effectively than Rome itself could. Outside Florence, however, there are remains of the early Tuscan or pre-Roman Etruscan civilisation (see **Cortona**, page 60; **Volterra**, page 76).

Guelf and Ghibelline

Florence emerged to prominence in the long series of wars and truces, alliances and betrayals, struggles and compromises, crimes and heroic deeds that began in Italy at the end of the 11th century. It was then that the first demarcations could be discerned of what was later called 'Guelf' and 'Ghibelline'. These were two factions in the struggle for control of the Holy Roman Empire. Guelfs were pro-papal (Florence was the leading city in Tuscany) and Ghibellines were pro-imperial (led by Pisa and Siena). These allegiances later became criss-crossed and confused, although Florence was always 'Guelf', that is to say, believed that her sovereign was the Pope, and not the Holy Roman Emperor. The Florentine connection to the Pope is vital to her history. Essentially, Florentine bankers funded the Guelf cause and grew rich when it won and the Emperor was pushed out of Italy. The stronger cities, like Florence, Pisa and Siena in Tuscany, besides Milan and Venice and many others in the north, became self-governing. The last Emperor to have real power in Italy was the mighty Frederick II, who died in 1250: his kingdom in the south of Italy was taken by Charles of Anjou in 1266, with an army blessed by the Pope but paid for by Florence. By this great Guelf victory, Florence's bankers doubled their money and her merchants won vital trade concessions. The city also had the security of the military protection of the powerful Angevin kings of Naples.

An extensive work on the upheavals of this time was written by Florence's most famous writer,

Dante Alighieri, father of Italian literature

8

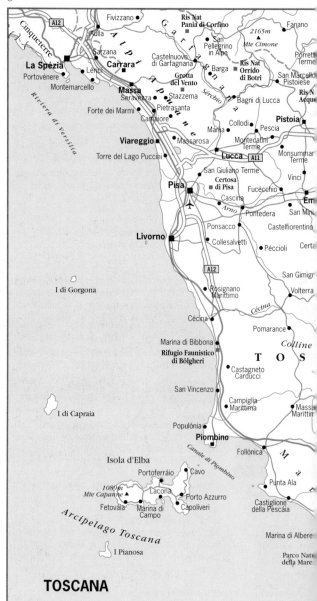

TOSCANA

0   20   40 km

I di Montecristo

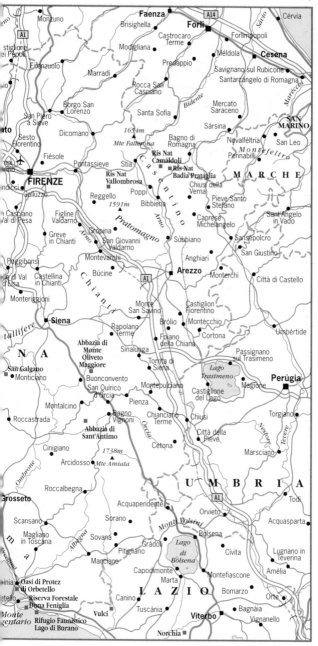

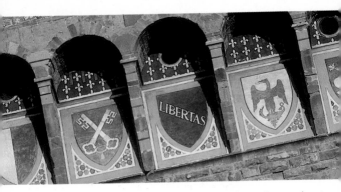

Detail from the Palazzo Vecchio overlooking the Piazza della Signoria

Dante Alighieri. Dante was born of a prominent Florentine family in 1265; he was exiled, following a violent division of the city into 'white' and 'black' Guelfs, in 1302. His *Divine Comedy* is not only a religious work but above all a political commentary, its famous *Inferno*, *Purgatorio* and *Paradiso* being populated by a wealth of historic and contemporary figures each of whom tells their story and explains their damning sin or saving virtue. This sometimes bitter and disillusioned poetic commentary on his own time, was written not in Latin, as was usual at the time, but in his own language, in the Tuscan dialect, and this, also used by Dante's younger contemporaries Petrarch (actually from Arezzo) and Boccaccio (from Certaldo near Florence), became the basis of written Italian during the Renaissance period and modern spoken Italian today. A visitor will soon discover, however, that despite the establishment of an Italian language in schools and the media, dialect is still very much alive, and Tuscan and Italian not at all the same thing. You will surely hear, for instance, the enormously aspirated 'h' to which many Tuscans convert hard 'c' (*casa*, house, becomes 'hasa') and the sweetly soft 'sh' for 'ci' or 'ce', giving you Bottishelli instead of Bottitchelli.

The free cities of Italy used their freedom, of course, to fight among themselves, while disguising their local politics under higher-sounding banners – thus Guelf Florence was opposed to Ghibelline Siena, but the true basis of their enmity was the friction of being competitive neighbours. Florence embarked on

a long struggle to subdue the lesser towns of
Tuscany – some, such as Arezzo and Cortona to
the east, without too much difficulty, others such
as Pisa and Lucca to the west and Siena to the
south, with varying or no success. To the north,
the Apennines formed a natural frontier with
Bologna. Pisa, also Ghibelline, was from early on
a very strong maritime power (her finest
monuments, the magnificent cathedral and the
Leaning Tower, were built at the height of her
power between the 11th and the 13th century),
but her harbour began silting up. Pisa was
eventually conquered by Florence in 1406, but
Lucca never was. Siena was a formidable rival
until the decimation of her population in the Black
Death of 1348. Siena began to decline but, even
so, did not become subject to Florence until
1555, after a heroic defence. By that time
Florence itself could no longer be called a self-
governing city, since it was ruled by the Dukes of
Tuscany, descendants of the Medici family. This
family of bankers had been the real power of the
republican city since 1434.

*Cosimo I, first
Medici Duke of
Tuscany*

The Age of the Medici

By the end of the 14th century, Florence was
firmly in control of her province, and although
Lucca and Siena remained independent they
were much smaller and less powerful.
Unfortunately, like so many other republican
cities, Florence was rent by all kinds of social
tensions – between the workers, the merchants
and the landowners, between different families of
the same class; between ambitious individuals.
In the 15th century, for the first time she evolved
a stable system of government under the Medici,
who ruled in effect but not in name – rather like
'godfathers'. The first of the Medici was the wily
Cosimo, known for his homely proverbs and his
diplomatic reticence; his son Piero was greatly
interested in art and his patronage helped to
make Florence the centre of the Italian
Renaissance or 're-birth' of classical learning in
art and architecture. Perhaps the most famous of
the Medici was Cosimo's grandson Lorenzo,
known as the Magnificent. He was himself a
skilled poet whose first love was literature,
though he also presided over a fantastic
flourishing of the arts, and in his gardens with

BACKGROUND

Giovanni de Medici

their classical sculptures the young Michelangelo studied. However, by the end of the 15th century signs of strain appeared: the Medici bank had financial difficulties, Italian politics were disrupted by a French invasion, and in 1494, two years after Lorenzo's death, the Medici were expelled. Towards the end of the 15th century a Dominican friar, Savonarola, was appointed prior of San Marco at Florence. With his fervent oratory, denouncing Church and State, he soon established a puritanical republic. However, when in 1496 he was excommunicated by Pope Alexander VI, the people quickly tired of his high ideals. Two years later he was accused of heresy and hanged. His body was then burnt. By 1532 Florence had ceased to be an independent republic, becoming instead the capital of the Grand Duchy of Tuscany.

The period of the High Renaissance, the early years of the 16th century, was one of great turmoil in Florence, as the city fought greater powers – France, the Holy Roman Emperor Charles V, the Pope – in a doomed effort to maintain sovereignty. At the same time, these years were the culmination of her art – during a blessed moment when Botticelli, Leonardo da Vinci, Raphael and Michelangelo were all working in Florence. The new turning-point was the successive election to the papacy of two members of the Medici family, as Leo X and Clement VII. In 1515 Leo X, second son of Lorenzo the Magnificent, triumphantly entered the city from which his elder brother had been expelled, and after a final flurry of resistance in 1530 (during which Michelangelo superintended the city's fortifications) the Medici dynasty of 'Dukes of Tuscany' was set up, supported by both Emperor and Pope and within the city by the garrison of the massive Fortezza da Basso, now used for trade exhibitions but originally very much more iron fist than velvet glove! The Medici dynasty, ably entrenched by Duke Cosimo I, conqueror of Siena, lasted with diminishing effectiveness and increasing scandal until 1737. Generally speaking, the arts and fortunes of Florence and Tuscany declined with them, although among the positive achievements of the Dukes was the creation of the port of Livorno to replace Pisa – otherwise known to

Englishmen on the Grand Tour in the 18th century as 'Leghorn'. Steps were taken, too, to improve the agriculture of southern Tuscany, the sparsely populated and marshy Maremma. With the death of Gian Gastone in 1737, rule passed to the more energetic Dukes of Lorena, temporarily ejected by Napoleon's invasion in 1799.

Finally in 1808 Tuscany, and Florence with it, was annexed to the French Empire. However, after the fall of Napoleon, Tuscany enjoyed a nominal independence during the Austrian dominance of Italy. The reigning Duke Leopold II departed more or less voluntarily as Florence joined the new state of Italy in 1859.

In 1865 Florence became the capital of the Kingdom of Italy and remained so until 1871. In World War II, Allied troops reached the outskirts of the city on 4 August 1944. On 11 August the Allies took Florence. The great monuments, most of which lie north of the River Arno, escaped undamaged because, although the Germans held the north bank, the British troops deliberately abstained from firing upon them. But

The statue of Neptune in the Piazza della Signoria

BACKGROUND

The church is still part of the city's daily life

the historic town itself received heavy damage. The heart of the old city round the Ponte Vecchio is gone. The actual bridge escaped serious harm, but the houses on it suffered severely from blast. By contrast the area which the Germans held against Allied attack remained relatively immune. Libraries and archives did not suffer. All the more important pictures had been removed to places of safety outside the city. Later however, in 1966, the art treasures and libraries of Florence suffered loss and damage when the Arno flooded the city, especially the low-lying Oltrarno. Visitors will see wall plaques at an amazing height, marking the levels the waters reached then and in earlier floods. The happy result of the worldwide effort of salvage was the training of a new generation of restorers who, during the last 25 years, have transformed the city's works of art. More recently, the political turmoil in Italy following the revelation during 1992 and 1993 of widespread corruption and Mafia involvement in the highest places reached a peak when a bomb was planted in the back streets behind the famous Uffizi Gallery, designed to inflict damage on its precious heritage of paintings. Fortunately the physical losses were marginal. Though Florence and its neighbouring cities have always been comparatively 'clean', they have by no means been left untarred by dirty stories of official bribery, and one conspicuous waste of money that had led to great anger among the Florentines was the long excavation and repaving of the Piazza Signoria in the late 1980s.

Art and Artists in Florence and Tuscany

The paintings, sculptures and buildings of the Renaissance are Florence's greatest glory, yet its immense artistic flowering – in the period from about 1400 to 1525 – had its roots in earlier centuries and more far-flung cities. Until the 12th century, Italian art had been dominated by the legacy of Byzantium, a heritage typified by the lovely but highly stylised world of icons and flat-faced Madonnas. About this time, the emergence of independent city states, new wealth and new learning brought an increasing sophistication. Some fresh or reinvented artistic language was needed to match the advances taking place in the civic and social domain. The first stirrings of this new language came in sculpture, and the work of **Nicola Pisano**, whose great pulpits in Pisa's Baptistery and the Duomo (Cathedral) in Siena took as their inspiration the realist reliefs of Greek and Roman sculpture. Such reworking of Classical forms was to be a cornerstone of Renaissance art, and one which Pisano's pupil, **Arnolfo di Cambio**, and his son **Giovanni Pisano** were to develop still further. Giovanni's work on the façade of Siena's cathedral, and the pulpits in Pistóia and Pisa, incorporated startling new positions for figures – designs and forms never seen in sculpture – and brought new vigour to formalised images; the Mother and Child ensemble, for example, began to suggest an emotional relationship in which maternal love was given an artistic expression.

Painting initially lagged some way behind sculpture's advances, but towards the end of the 13th century, it too began to shake off the hidebound strictures of Byzantine art. The change started in Rome, where artists like **Pietro Cavallini** turned from mosaic – very much a Byzantine tradition – to fresco, where water-colour is painted on to damp plaster. This medium was more able to match sculpture's new realism and more complex compositions. With others, the Florentine **Cimabue**, described by Vasari as the 'father of Italian painting', furthered the move towards naturalism with work in Assisi's Basilica of St Francis. By far the most important figure of the 14th century was his fellow Florentine, **Giotto di Bondone**.

The spectacular ceiling in Santa Maria del Carmine

Unfortunately much of Giotto's painting is lost, though some survives in Padua and Florence (in Santa Croce's Bardi and Perruzzi chapels). It revolutionised Italian art, forging a new style independent both of Byzantine and of French Gothic art. Giotto's images had new depth, space, foreshortening, light and shade – and turned to the real world for subject and inspiration. For the first time, people capable of real movement and emotion were set in backgrounds with naturalistic details – birds, clothes and so forth. In time, Giotto's disciples – **Maso di Banco, Agnolo di Gaddi, Bernardo Daddi, Giovanni da Milano** – began to work in the master's style around Florence's churches.

The Sienese School

Although Giotto was to be immensely influential, and set a firm artistic course for the Renaissance, it was the less innovative Sienese who made the running for much of the 14th century. **Duccio di Buoninsegna** was the School's founding father, adapting Byzantine motifs to his own brilliant use of colour and design. Goldleaf, vivid reds and brilliant blues dominate the lovely narrative *tempera* (pigment mixed with egg yolk) panels of his greatest work, the high altarpiece of Siena Cathedral now preserved in the nearby Museo dell' Opera del Duomo. Duccio's followers, above all **Simone Martini**, combined his legacy with the space and depth of Giotto to create a style of immense influence, not only in Italy but also in France and even the Netherlands and England. Simone left to work in Avignon at the papal court, but beforehand produced most notably a portrait of *Guidoriccio da Foliagno* in Siena's Palazzo Pubblico, and an *Annunciation* (in the Uffizi), painted with his brother-in-law, **Lippo Memmi**. Equally sweet and exquisitely lyrical was **Ambrogio Lorenzetti** who with his brother, **Pietro Lorenzetti**, also painted buildings and landscapes in a new way. These advances are encapsulated in *The Allegory of Good and Bad Government* (in Siena's Palazzo Pubblico), one of Italy's earliest surviving secular frescos.

The Early Renaissance

A mood of intellectual and artistic ferment came to glorious fruition – especially in Florence – during the 15th century. Humanist scholarship, and a revival of the Classical ideal in art, played

Santa Maria Novella is renowned for its beautiful frescos

a key role, as did the wealth of Florence, by then a thriving and cosmopolitan city. Individual genius flourished in its free-thinking atmosphere, enriched by the exchange of ideas among many artists working together drawn by its booming artistic reputation.

Although one of the features of the age was the close relationship between the arts – painters were often also sculptors and architects – three early artists stand out in each of the main disciplines. **Filippo Brunelleschi** triumphed as an architect, throwing a dome over Florence's cathedral by returning to Roman principles, but also clarifying ideals of design and advancing the new science of perspective. Greatest of the century's sculptors was **Donatello**, an elusive character who produced staggeringly innovative work, returning the nude to the mainstream of artistic expression (the bronze *David* in Florence's Bargello), and using a variety of media (stone, wood, bronze, terracotta) for his emotional and intensely passionate work. Third of the triumvirate was **Masaccio**, a master of perspective. So perfect – and new – was his handling of depth, that Florentines are said to have besieged Santa Maria Novella church for days, eager to see but unable to believe that his *Trinity* was painted on a solid wall. Masaccio's close collaborator, **Masolino da Panicale**, with whom he worked on the fresco cycle in Brancacci chapel in Florence's Santa Maria del Carmine, was less revolutionary, and few artists who followed were able or willing to pursue Masaccio's rigorous principles, tending to sweeten and prettify his powerful style. At least until there came Michelangelo!

Filippo Brunelleschi, creator of the Duomo's dome

As the many ingredients of earlier artistic endeavour were thrown into Florence's great melting pot, these three artists unleashed the full weight of what was to become known as the Renaissance. A date, as far as a date can be fixed, for the start of this *rinascita*, or rebirth, is often fixed at 1401, with the public competition to design a second door for the Baptistery in Florence's Piazza del Duomo. **Lorenzo Ghiberti** emerged as the winner; a sculptor under strong French Gothic influence but increasingly, as he worked on his two successive sets of doors for the Battistero, up-to-date with Renaissance forms. Another notable sculptor was **Luca della Robbia**, who perfected the art of glazed terracotta, which his family later spread, very profitably, across much of Tuscany.

Nowhere does the Renaissance avalanche of names become more overwhelming than among the painters. Many were innovators, some only accomplished copyists, but all were responsible for the beautiful body of work with which the period (also known as the Quattrocento) is most commonly associated. One of the earliest, **Paolo Uccello** was also one of the most obsessed with the possibilities of perspective, driving himself to personal and artistic eccentricity with the new-found obsession. Challenging, almost visionary work was the result, best seen in Santa Maria Novella's *Noah* and the *Battle of San Romano* in the Uffizi. Equally intense, but on a more mystical, religious plane, was the heavenly inspiration of **Fra Angelico**, a devout Dominican friar. His sublime work, intended as an aid to devotion, was innovative in composition and colour. Few matched the inimitable and ethereal blue of his palette, best seen in the frescos of his own monastery, San Marco. Less profound, and 'more enamoured of earth' was his pupil **Benozzo Gozzoli**, who left examples of his light, but beautifully decorated work all over Tuscany and Central Italy.

More in keeping with the mystery and depth of Fra Angelico, if not his religious devotion, was **Fra Filippo Lippi** (he had an illegitimate child by a nun). Soon abandoning his master, Masaccio, he moved into new areas, with complex compositional groups, detailed colouring and mystical paintings of poetic landscape and wistful Madonnas. Another spur to artistic progress came from the versatile **Antonio Pollaiuolo**, painter, engraver, sculptor and goldsmith, who grappled with the problems of anatomy and movement. He also undertook a wide range of commissions, both secular and religious, exemplifying the ever-widening interests of artists and patrons as the 15th century advanced. **Andrea del Verrocchio** formed part of this trend: a fine, multi-talented artist in his own right, but better known as a teacher and, like Pollaiuolo, the head of a flourishing workshop.

Luca della Robbia's development of terracotta glazing landed his family in the money

Galleria dell'
Accademia or bust

As the century progressed, spawning increasing numbers of artists, such as **Domenico Veneziano, Andrea del Castagno, Domenico Ghirlandaio**, it also moved towards its artistic climax, heralded first by **Sandro Botticelli**. Though his works stand alone, he exemplified the early Florentine Renaissance mastery of graceful, expressive line, his paintings a dazzling vision of entrancing silhouettes. The literary humanism sponsored by the Medici was responsible for the mythological themes that characterise his most famous paintings. Next to him stands the figure of **Leonardo da Vinci**, the paragon of the Florentine Quattrocento, a 'universal genius' trained in Verrocchio's workshop, excelling in virtually everything to which he put his hand. Little of his output, however, remains in Florence or Tuscany.

The High Renaissance

Leonardo's *Last Supper* in Milan's Santa Maria delle Grazie is usually considered to have been the first masterpiece of the so-called High Renaissance, the climactic end of the era. It also reminds us that Florence did not have a monopoly either on artistic talent or execution. **Piero della Francesca**, from the tiny Tuscan town of Sansepolcro, was a singular artist deeply preoccupied by perspective and the mathematics of composition. In Cortona, his

BACKGROUND

Giovanni de Paolo was a late exponent of the Sienese school

pupil **Luca Signorelli** exerted enormous influence on the painters who followed him. In Siena, old traditions continued to appeal, but were mingled with the new learning of Florence. The city's finest artist was the sculptor **Jacopo della Quercia**, but there were also painters – **Sassetta** and **Giovanni di Paolo** – who took some heed of Florentine innovation.

At the turn of the 15th century, however, Florence and Tuscany began to lose their artistic primacy, and the tenets of early Renaissance painting gave way to new ideas and directions. Above this change towered **Michelangelo**, with Leonardo, the age's consummate genius. Concerned primarily with the nude and the heroic figure, his work is represented in Florence where he spent the earlier part of his career, by the *David*, the *Pietà* and the Medici tombs. Artists such as **Raphael** continued to study in the city, but by about 1525, against a background of political collapse, it ceased to be the crucible of artistic endeavour.

Nonetheless, homegrown artists continued to excel, in particular exponents of Mannerism which put art above nature, style above substance, and flouted the conventions of colour, scale and composition. Its leading Florentine lights were **Rosso Fiorentino** and **Jacopo Pontormo**. **Andrea del Sarto** and **Agnolo Bronzino** shared the preoccupation with colour, but worked slightly more within the classical mainstream. Bronzino, in particular, is remembered for his portraits of the rich and famous, works that in the future were to have considerable influence on the genre. Thereafter, with one or two honourable exceptions, Florentine artists fell into decline, and decadence. In the following centuries the city no longer led the development of style – though in the Palazzo Pitti there are fine ceilings in Roman baroque style, and in the 17th century **Cato Dolci** produced exquisite Raphael-like Madonnas. In the 18th century the city became a stopping point on the Grand Tour, gradually becoming *the* Italian Old Master capital as 19th-century taste became 'pre-Raphaelite'; Botticelli's popularity rose again with the rise of Art Nouveau, which favoured the same sinuous forms and lack of realism.

WHAT TO SEE IN FLORENCE

The visitor is not exactly short of sights to see in Florence. The city offers a bewildering number of sights to the visitor – some 400 palaces, 50 ancient churches and 70 museums alone – and the dedicated sightseer is at severe risk of contracting Stendhal's Syndrome, first recorded when the famous 19th-century French writer suffered dizzy spells brought on by an overdose of Florentine beauty! To avoid this fate, bouts of sightseeing should be liberally balanced with siestas, random strolls through the winding streets in search of nothing more demanding than local colour, and frequent pit-stops for a glass of Chianti or an *espresso*. The last is particularly important during summer when the intense heat can drive the doughtiest sightseer to distraction.

The city has a habit of revealing more treasures the more you see, and then there are the outlying villages, churches and small towns of Tuscany! Whether you are a casual or a dedicated sightseer, it is important to plan your time with some care (hence nearby sights are given beside the location in the following pages). At the same time you must not be too rigid, for it is almost unknown to have 100 per cent success in seeing what you want to see. There are two major obstacles, which you can do nothing about. The first is restoration, which will have removed a picture for cleaning or locked a building or shrouded it with scaffolding

Brunelleschi's unique landmark

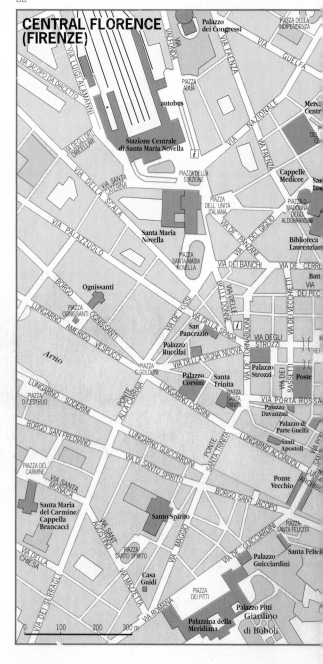

CENTRAL FLORENCE (FIRENZE)

PIAZZA DELLA INDIPENDENZA

Palazzo dei Congressi

VIA VALFONDA

VIA LUIGI ALAMANNI

VIA JACOPO DA DIACETO

VIA FAENZA

VIA GUELFA

PIAZZA ADUA

autobus

Merca Centr

VIA NAZIONALE

VIA DEGLI ORTI ORICELLARI

Stazione Centrale di Santa Maria Novella

VIA FAENZA

DEL CE

i

PIAZZA DELLA STAZIONE

VIA DELLA SCALA

VIA SANTA CATERINA

PIAZZA DELL' UNITÀ ITALIANA

Cappelle Medicee

San Lo

VIA PALAZZUOLO

Santa Maria Novella

VIA DE' PANZANI

PIAZZA D. MADONNA DEGLI ALDOBRANDINI

Biblioteca Laurenzian

VIA DEL GIGLIO

PIAZZA SANTA MARIA NOVELLA

VIA DEI BANCHI

VIA DE ' CERRE

BORGO

Ognissanti

VIA DELLE BELLE DONNE

Batt VIA DEI PEC

PIAZZA OGNISSANTI

OGNISSANTI

VIA DE' FOSSI

VIA DELLA SPADA

VIA DE' VECCHIETTI

LUNGARNO AMERIGO VESPUCCI

San Pancrazio

i

Arno

Palazzo Rucellai

VIA DELLA VIGNA NUOVA

VIA DEGLI STROZZI

PIAZZA C. GOLDONI

VIA DE' TORNABUONI

VIA DEI SASSETTI

REF

Palazzo Corsini

Palazzo Strozzi

LUNGARNO CORSINI

Santa Trinita

Poste

LUNGARNO SODERINI

PIAZZA D. CESTELLO

PONTE ALLA CARRAIA

PIAZZA SANTA TRINITA

VIA PORTA ROSSA

Palazzo Davanzati

BORGO SAN FREDIANO

LUNGARNO GUICCIARDINI

PONTE SANTA TRINITA

LUNGARNO ACCIAIUOLI

Palazzo di Parte Guelfa

Santi Apostoli

LUNG ARCHIBU

VIA DI SANTO SPIRITO

PIAZZA DEL CARMINE

VIA SANTA MONACA

BORGO SANT JACOPO

Ponte Vecchio

PIAZZA SANTA FELICITA

Santa Maria del Carmine/ Cappella Brancacci

VIA SANT' AGOSTINO

Santo Spirito

VIA MAGGIO

VIA DE' GUICCIARDINI

Santa Felici

PIAZZA SANTO SPIRITO

VIA DELLA CHIESA

Casa Guidi

Palazzo Guicciardini

VIA MAZZETTA

PIAZZA DEI PITTI

Palazzo Pitti Giardino di Boboli

VIA DEI SERRAGLI

VIA ROMANA

Palazzina della Meridiana

0   100   200   300 m

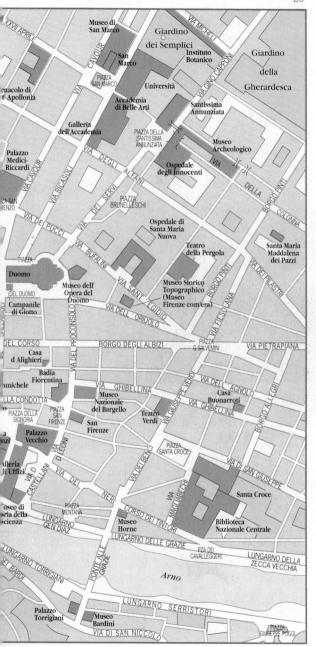

Front row seats for the sights

(here you must console yourself that it will eventually emerge transformed, like Masaccio's Brancacci Chapel in 1990). The second is a strike or time taken off by personnel, liable to happen at any time, without notice. A possible third is the exorbitant price you have to pay to visit the museums these days (but not **Senior Citizens** – see **Directory**), and the long queues that form. Most of the museums close on Mondays, incidentally, and on some, not all, holidays (see **Holidays** in the **Directory**). One final tip: *get up early* and see what you most want to see in the morning!

Areas of the City

Central Florence

The heart of Florence lies on the north bank of River Arno, centred on three magnificent piazzas. Piazza del Duomo is the historic religious focus of the city, dominated by the twin jewels of the cathedral – Giotto's campanile, and Brunelleschi's inspired dome rising above the ordered geometry of the green and white marble church and press of ancient buildings 'like a captive balloon', in the words of Mark Twain. Heading south towards the Arno, Piazza della Repubblica was the site of the Roman Forum, then the Mercato Vecchio, the principal market, founded in the 14th century. However, the Piazza was a 19th-century creation, and involved the destruction of old buildings and streets by then slums. The old heart of the city, and still the centre of political demonstrations today, was the Piazza della Signoria, outside the Palazzo Vecchio (the government house of republican Florence). Here the heads of Florence's leading families, the *signori*, governed the city, and in this square the 15th-century republican heretic Savonarola was burnt at the stake. The square is now graced with a grand selection of monumental statuary, and fronts the priceless collections of the Uffizi Gallery. South of the Uffizi, the Arno, spanned by a series of bridges, divides the city in two. The medieval Ponte Vecchio was the only bridge to survive World War II, though the Ponte Santa Trinità was rebuilt with masonry dredged from the river.

Il Bargello and Santa Croce

East of Piazza della Signoria, among a maze of narrow medieval streets packed with dusty workshops, there is a handful of palace-museums and the austere façade of the former Bargello prison. The prison now houses a fine sculpture collection, but its gory history has been translated into neighbouring street names such as Via dei Malcontenti (Street of the Miserable) which led from the dungeons to the public gallows at Piazza Piave. It is a short walk further east from the Bargello and south towards the Arno to another Florentine ecclesiastical marvel, the church of Santa Croce. A generously proportioned, 13th-century Franciscan foundation, Santa Croce is filled with monuments to the great from Petrarch and Dante to Michelangelo, Machiavelli and Rossini.

The Medici Quarter

Though Florence abounds with monuments to the 300 years of Medici rule, and Medici palaces are scattered throughout the city and up into the hills, the enclave north of the cathedral is the historic heartland of Florence's First Family. It is an area of great contrast where imposing memorials to old money are under siege from the daily progress of life in one of the less salubrious areas of town, where the stolid façade of the Palazzo Medici appears bleak and rather dull above the colour and bustle of the modern market in Piazza San Lorenzo. Across the piazza, the Renaissance charm of the Basilica di San Lorenzo is crowned by an elegant scaled-down Brunelleschi dome and the interior contains the opulent Medici chapels filled with works by Michelangelo. Just north of the basilica, the covered Mercato Centrale (Central Market) has mountains of gleaming fresh fruit and vegetables, Tuscan hams and cheeses. Follow Via Cavour north to the university district and Piazza San Marco for further notable museums. The Museo di San Marco is housed in a convent built with funds from Cosimo de Medici, and the Museo Archeologico is one of the finest in Italy.

WHAT TO SEE

Santa Maria Novella and Le Cascine

West of the city centre, the elegant façade of Santa Maria Novella lends a touch of antique charm to the largely modern area around the central station. The church's interior is lavishly decorated with carvings and frescos paid for by influential families like the Strozzi or the Tornabuoni. Heading southeast, Piazza Ognissanti is sandwiched between the Arno and the Ognissanti church which contains 15th-century works of art commissioned by the Vespucci family. West, along the banks of the Arno, the 300-acre Cascine park was once a Medici estate, but now offers a wealth of sporting facilities and hosts the *Festa di Grillo* on Ascension Day, when crickets are caught and caged for the day.

Oltrarno

Literally translated as 'beyond the Arno', the Oltrarno district on the left bank of the Arno was first incorporated into the city during the 13th century. It has a long tradition as an artisans' quarter, but also boasts some of the oldest and grandest Florentine edifices. These include the sprawling Palazzo Pitti founded by the Pitti family in an attempt to challenge the Medici monopoly on monumental building projects. Eventually the Medici bought them out, and the palace now houses a series of fine museums, backed by the Boboli Gardens. Notable ecclesiastical sites include Santa Felicità, Brunelleschi's Santo Spirito, and the superb Brancacci Chapel of Santa Maria del Carmine with frescos by Masaccio. For a panoramic view, follow the scenic four-mile (6km) route of the Viale dei Colli to Piazzale Michelangelo on the slopes of San Miniato.

ACCADEMIA *see* GALLERIA DELL'ACCADEMIA

◆
BADIA FIORENTINA (FLORENCE ABBEY)

Via del Proconsolo
(near **Bargello**, **Palazzo Vecchio**)
This rather piecemeal church and the adjoining cloisters has 15th-century tombs and some paintings worth seeing, such as Filippino Lippi's *St Bernard*.
Open: daily 09.00 to 12.00hrs, 16.00 to 18.00hrs.

Badia Fiorentina, between the Duomo and the Arno

BARGELLO (NATIONAL MUSEUM FOR SCULPTURE)
Via del Proconsolo 4
(near **Palazzo Vecchio**, **Badia Fiorentina**)

The original purpose of the massive Bargello building was as a law-court and prison, a kind of fortress of public order. The artist Andrea del Castagno earned his nickname 'Andrea degli Impiccati', Andrew of the Hanged Men, after receiving his first 'break' here, aged 20 – a commission to paint frescos of hanged wrongdoers or traitors on its walls. He had as his models the actual hanged bodies, while they could be kept on display. It was meant to be a grim place. It now houses some of the greatest sculptures of the Florentine Renaissance.

On the ground floor opposite the entrance is the 16th Century Room, with such important works as Michelangelo's very drunk, tottering *Bacchus* and round (*tondo*) relief *Madonna*, and others by the greatest sculptors working for the Medici dukes, up to and including Giambologna. Above, reached by the outside stairs, is the 15th Century Room, which has several masterpieces by Donatello, including the early marble *David*, the extraordinary slim, naked, bronze *David*, the brilliantly alert *St George* (transferred here from **Orsanmichele**), and the dancing so-called *Amor-Atys* (nobody knows quite who he is). Also of interest are the two reliefs by Ghiberti and Brunelleschi that came first and second in the competition of 1401 for the bronze doors of the **Battistero**. It is interesting to consider this crucial decision determining the subsequent course of the Renaissance: Ghiberti is prettier and more elegant; Brunelleschi more forceful and expressive, and it is perhaps surprising that he did not win. However, Ghiberti used considerably less weight of bronze than Brunelleschi!

Do not neglect the other rooms. Adjoining the Early Renaissance Room are bronzes of animals done in the later 16th century, when there was a great vogue for them, and also an important collection of statuettes. Though now rather dead in their glass cases, these were the objects Renaissance patrons actually handled and spent their private money on – for pleasure, not for God or public appearances. More are upstairs by the internal stairs on the second floor, along with a collection of ceramics including Della Robbia faience (a Renaissance invention, a secret of great importance because it provided both bright and lasting colours, it has been kept by the Della Robbia family) and of majolica. The statuettes include Pollaiuolo's justly famous *Hercules and Antaeus* (who drew strength from his mother the Earth; Hercules had to kill him by lifting him up and squeezing him to death). Beside this, there are some wonderfully vigorous male busts and some very beautiful female ones, notably by Verrocchio.

On the first floor again, continuing round, the room of the Carrand Bequest contains a large number of disparate

Michelangelo's David *in the Galleria dell' Accademia*

*Renaissance skill and devotion in
the Battistero's brazen doors*

objects, from Byzantine ivories to
Renaissance table knives.
Open: Tuesday to Saturday 09.00
to 14.00hrs, Sunday and holidays
09.00 to 13.00hrs.
Closed: Monday.

◆◆
BATTISTERO SAN GIOVANNI (BAPTISTERY)
Piazza San Giovanni
(opposite the **Duomo**)
The Baptistery was the navel of
medieval and Renaissance
Florence – when communal
baptisms were carried out you in
effect registered your children as
citizens. It was also believed that
it had been converted from a
temple of Mars and was the
oldest building in Florence. In
fact it is Romanesque, of the 10th
or 11th century. But Brunelleschi
drew inspiration from it when he
came to develop his specially
Florentine, 'old-style'
Renaissance architecture
(breaking with 'modern' Gothic –
as it was then), as can be seen in
the details of his **Ospedale**.
The glory of the Baptistery lies in
its three sets of bronze doors:
each was originally made for the
main entrance facing the
cathedral, but was displaced to a
side portal by the next one. The
first was the present entrance
door, made by Andrea Pisano in
the 1330s in a severe, clear style
modelled on Giotto's painting.
The next was Ghiberti's of 1402–
1425, the commission he won
against a shortlist of five sculptors
including Brunelleschi, the
runner-up, and Jacopo della
Quercia from Siena. (See

Ghiberti's and Brunelleschi's
original competition entries in the
Bargello, page 27). These first
doors by Ghiberti are obviously

commissioned from Ghiberti another set of doors, which took him another 25 years. These 'doors of Paradise' (the description is attributed to Michelangelo) were done, however, to Ghiberti's own design, which could demonstrate much better the new game of perspective. They have now been replaced by a replica and are housed in the **Museo dell'Opera del Duomo**. Also worth a look, over the side doors, are early 16th-century sculptures, one by Rustici who may have been advised by Leonardo.

Inside, the mosaics of the vault were by Venetians 'borrowed' by the Florentines because the art had died out in Central Italy in the 13th century. The tomb of the 15th-century schismatic Pope John XXIII, a Florentine (who decently resigned in order to resolve the schism), is by Donatello and Michelozzo, an outstanding landmark of early Renaissance style. *Open*: Monday to Saturday 13.00 to 18.00hrs, Sunday 09.00 to 13.00hrs.

◆
BELVEDERE (FORTE DI BELVEDERE)
Via de San Leonardo
(near **Giardino di Bóboli**)
On a fine day this is an excellent point to walk to (through the **Boboli Gardens** if you like) to look out over Florence; there is also a café open in summer and during the exhibitions held here. The fort was built by the Medici dukes as a repressive partner to the Fortezza da Basso and as a refuge in case of revolt (see **Ponte Vecchio**, page 43).
Open: daily 09.00 to 20.00hrs.

imitations of Andrea Pisano's, but done with much more grace and virtuosity. So pleased were the authorities that they immediately

◆◆◆
CAPPELLE MEDICÉE (MEDICI CHAPELS) ✓

Piazza Madonna degli Aldobrandini
(at the rear of **San Lorenzo**, near **Palazzo Medici**)

These 16th-century Medici chapels are really the continuation of the 15th-century Medici chapels on the left side of San Lorenzo, and Michelangelo's New Sacristy on the right side is the symmetrical equivalent of the Old Sacristy on the left. Indeed it actually opens on to the church, but the door is closed and you have to gain entry through the crypt at the rear, where you have also to pay! The sensible thing to do is to see the church and Old Sacristy first, and then the Michelangelo. Michelangelo in fact clearly respected the lines of Brunelleschi's Old Sacristy even though he transformed its architecture. He seems originally to have intended (in 1520) a central free-standing monument, but evolved this unique arrangement in his usual way, ever dissatisfied with first thoughts. The tombs are those of the ruling branch of the Medici

Lorenzo de Medici: the Magnificent

family who had not been commemorated to date, namely Lorenzo the Magnificent, his brother Giuliano, his son Giuliano (Duke of Nemours) and his grandson Lorenzo (Duke of Urbino). However, only the two Dukes' tombs were completed (in 1534), together with a *Madonna* (the two flanking saints are by pupils). And their scene is stolen by the figures draped so awkwardly on their tombs, of *Night*, *Day*, *Dusk* and *Dawn*, who have no further meaning but were vehicles of Michelangelo's titanic emotions.

Most people just march through the last and grandest of the Medici Chapels. The great domed one with unbelievably rich coloured marble decoration, designed by Buontalenti in the closing years of the 16th century. But it is one of the earliest and most important examples of that kind of taste, and the last influential work of art made in Florence. *Open*: Tuesday to Saturday 09.00 to 14.00hrs. Sunday and holidays 09.00 to 13.00hrs. *Closed*: Monday.

Buontalenti's Medici Chapel

Ornate decoration on the Duomo

CONTINI BONACOSSI
COLLECTION *see* GIARDINO
DI BÓBOLI

DAVANZATI PALACE *see*
MUSEO DELL'ANTICA CASA
FIORENTINA

◆
DUOMO (CATHEDRAL OF
SANTA MARIA DEL FIORE)
A close view is not the best thing
about the cathedral: it is better
from a distance, either from a
height above the surrounding
city or looking along side streets
to glimpse a segment of its great
looming dome. Inside it is largely
empty of its works of art – now in
the **Museo dell'Opera del
Duomo** – and there remain only
the two frescos, by Paolo Uccello
and Andrea del Castagno, of a
couple of army captains who
won victories when fighting for
Florence. One of them is an
Englishman, John Hawkwood,
who hardly deserves the
memorial: he fought for anybody
and everybody, and if nobody
employed him and his band he
wandered the peninsula looting
anyway. Uccello also painted the
absurd faces round the clock
inside the west façade wall, but
now that the restoration of the
Brancacci Chapel (see **Santa
Maria del Carmine**, page 51)
has brought to light two new
decorative heads by the window,
you can see what Uccellos' were
based on. At the east end, a set
of bronze doors by Luca della
Robbia can be compared with
those by his contemporaries
Ghiberti on the **Battistero** or
those by Donatello in the Old

CARMINE *see* SANTA MARIA
DEL CARMINE

◆◆
CASA BUONARROTI
(MICHELANGELO MUSEUM)
Via Ghibellina 70
(near **Santa Croce**)
There are two stupendous early
works by the master in this small
museum, as well as a collection
of drawings (shown only in
reproductions) and a large
contemporary wooden model of
Michelangelo's unexecuted
design for the church of San
Lorenzo, and finally some odd
paintings.
The stupendous early works on
display are the *Madonna della
Scala* ('of the stair'), a *tondo* or
round relief, and the *Battle of the
Centaurs*, another relief, and
they justify the visit. There is also
a crucifix attributed to the
adolescent genius.
Open: Wednesday to Monday
09.30 to 13.30hrs.
Closed: Tuesday.

CATHEDRAL *see* DUOMO

sacristy in **San Lorenzo**. The crypt (remains of Santa Reparata Church) can also be visited. *Open*: Monday to Saturday 10.30 to 17.00hrs.
Closed: Sunday.
But the cathedral is most famous for its dome, the work that made its designer and engineer, Brunelleschi, famous throughout Italy, and proved the Renaissance was something more than a new style. In its original design the Cathedral had been a conventional basilica, but competition with their neighbours (for instance, Siena) led the Florentines to project a much wider dome than first intended. The difficulty was, how to vault it. It is 140 feet (42m) wide and 180 feet (55m) high. Brunelleschi solved the problem by reviving the ancient Roman technique of building upwards in ever decreasing rings, though the egg-shaped dome with its Gothic ribs makes no attempt to imitate Roman buildings – rather it repeats the outline of the Baptistery beside it. Currently the dome is still under restoration, but the tour up between the two skins of the dome to the lantern – only for those not afraid of a lot of steps nor of horribly vertiginous heights – is available (not Sunday). The dome was not finally completed until 1461 but was substantially in place before Brunelleschi's death in 1436, by which time sculpture to decorate the Cathedral was already proceeding apace. Most of this is in the **Museo dell'Opera del Duomo** but one work by Donatello's rival Nanni di Banco is just inside the right-hand façade door, and another by Nanni, unfortunately not yet cleaned from its grime, is outside on the left of the nave: *The Assumption of the Virgin*. However, cleaning of the façade, most of which is 19th-century though in harmony with the rest of the 14th-century nave, is approaching completion. (*Open*: daily 10.00 to 17.00hrs.) Also 14th-century is the **Campanile** or bell-tower – the design is attributed to Giotto – which can be climbed as well. On the outside, it has replicas of some interesting reliefs of the *Arti* or trades of Florence, and of the standing statues by Donatello and others, made for this position. The originals are in the **Museo dell'Opera del Duomo**. *Open*: daily 10.00 to 17.00hrs.

◆
GALLERIA DELL'ACCADEMIA
Via Ricasoli 60
(near **San Marco**, **Santissima Annunziata**, **Cenacolo di Sant'Apollonia**, **Museo Archeologico**)
The Accademia is housed in the large rooms of the hospital of St Matthew. It was founded in 1784 by Grand Duke Pietro Leopoldo I of Lorraine.
The one star above is a terrible heresy, because the Accademia is always ranked as one of the great museums in Florence. That is virtually for only one reason: because it has a collection of sculptures by Michelangelo including his *David* (a replica has been put in its original place outside the Palazzo Vecchio). You pay a whopping admission if that is all you have come to see. It also has four *Slaves* by

Michelangelo made for Pope Julius II's tomb and *St Matthew* for Florence Cathedral, all magnificent, unfinished, straining figures, in marked contrast to the composure of *David*. The collection of pictures is much less important but includes some early Renaissance works of the Florentine school and a *Madonna* by Botticelli.

Open: Tuesday to Saturday 09.00 to 14.00hrs; Sunday and holidays 09.00 to 13.00hrs.
Closed: Monday.

◆
GIARDINO DI BÓBOLI (BOBOLI GARDENS)
Piazza de'Pitti
(entrance through **Palazzo Pitti**) The Boboli Gardens are ornamental pleasure gardens (with perhaps too much uphill walking for some) laid out in the mid-16th century when the Medici had adopted the Palazzo Pitti as a residence. (See also **Belvedere**, page 30.)

The gardens house a number of museums (besides the Pitti and the exhibition space of the Belvedere). These are the **Museo delle Porcellane** (Museum of Porcelain), the **Galleria del Costume** (Gallery of Costume) and the **Contini Bonacossi collection**. The first two may make a welcome change from pictures and sculptures, while the Contini Bonacossi bequest is something of a must for anyone seriously interested in Early Renaissance art: it has some first-quality things. For the first two, entrance tickets at the **Museo degli Argenti** (Silver Museum) in the Palazzo de'Pitti; for the **Contini**

Bonacossi, appointments at the **Uffizi** (tel: 218341).
Open: Tuesday to Sunday 09.00 to 19.30hrs (June to August); earlier closing rest of year.
Closed: Sunday.

LOGGIA DEI LANZI
Piazza della Signoria
(near **Uffizi**, **Palazzo Vecchio**) Loggias like this were common in the Middle Ages but were disappearing from the city in Renaissance times. Originally serving as informal meeting places, this loggia was converted by the Medici dukes into a sculpture gallery housing Cellini's bronze *Perseus*, a Mannerist masterpiece of minor detail, and Giambologna's *Rape of the Sabine*, a deliberate attempt to out-Michelangelo Michelangelo.

MEDICI CHAPEL *see* CAPPELLE MEDICÉE

MUSEO ARCHEOLOGICO (ARCHAEOLOGICAL MUSEUM)
Via della Colonna 36
(near **Santissima Annunziata**, **Accademia**, **San Marco**) Works are still going on in the Museo Archeologico, but some rooms have emerged, including those of the most important aspect of the collection, the Etruscan pieces. Another section of interest is that displaying jewels and cameos, many once in the Medici collection: these little images sold for immense prices in the Renaissance and have some importance for Renaissance art (for instance the flying winds of Botticelli's *Birth of*

Venus were imitated from one). The enormous collection encompasses Greek and Roman and also Egyptian objects.
Open: Tuesday to Saturday 09.00 to 14.00hrs, Sunday and holidays 09.00 to 13.00hrs.

♦♦
MUSEO DELL'ANTICA CASA FIORENTINA (OLD FLORENTINE HOUSE MUSEUM)
Palazzo Davanzati, Via Porta Rossa 13
(near **Orsanmichele**)
The Davanzati Palace is a mid-14th-century building that preserves some of its original decoration and has been restored with Renaissance furniture. It is therefore a fascinating glimpse into the way of life and context of the late Middle Ages and Early Renaissance period in Florence. From its outside staircase to its upstairs kitchen and a bedroom decorated with scenes from a chivalric romance, there is a great deal to see.
Open: Tuesday to Saturday 09.00 to 14.00hrs; Sunday until 13.00hrs.
Closed: Monday.

♦♦
MUSEO DELL'OPERA DEL DUOMO (CATHEDRAL MUSEUM)
Piazza Duomo 9
(behind the **Duomo**)
The museum houses works of sculpture formerly in or around the Cathedral. On the ground floor, three magnificent sculptures of the *Evangelists* from the façade of the Cathedral, even though it was far from finished at that time (1408–15). The arrangement was, in the typical competitive spirit of the Early Renaissance, that Donatello, Nanni di Banco and a certain Ciuffagni should each carve one Evangelist, and whoever did the best should carve the fourth. However, Ciuffagni evidently peeped at Donatello's, and in fact a record survives in which Donatello requests that a lock be put on his workshop door – presumably to stop him peeping. But in the end the fourth Evangelist was given to someone else again. Also on this floor, a *Madonna* by Arnolfo di Cambio, first architect of the Cathedral (*c*1296); wooden models; tools

Museo dell'Opera del Duomo

WHAT TO SEE

and more sculpture. On the way up the stairs, Michelangelo's moving *Pietà*, with a self-portrait in the head of Nicodemus and an inferior Mary Magdalen by another hand attempting to patch up the job after Michelangelo had broken it and abandoned it. On the first floor, two Singing Galleries, one by Donatello, the other by Luca della Robbia. Luca's was the earlier, beautifully carved in a pure white marble; after first attempting something similar (panels he used instead at Prato Cathedral) Donatello decided on a much more dramatic arrangement. In the same room, some highly expressive statues originally on the Campanile of the **Duomo**, and Donatello's *Mary Magdalene* in wood, showing her after fasting and praying long weeks in the desert following Christ's death. The originals of the 'trades' from the Campanile are in the adjacent room.

In the last room, panels from the 'Paradise' **Battistero** doors are displayed. The silver altar was made by Pollaiuolo and Verrocchio, and the embroidered vestments were designed by Pollaiuolo. Both are important examples of Renaissance art about 1470.
Open: Monday to Saturday 09.00 to 19.30hrs (18.00 winter).
Closed: Sunday.

◆

MUSEO DI STORIA DELLA SCIENZA (HISTORY OF SCIENCE MUSEUM)
Piazza dei Giudici 1
(near **Uffizi**)
This museum reveals the state of technology during the heyday of Florentine art, and in those days science and art went together – witness Leonardo. The real hero of the museum is, however, not Leonardo but Galileo. It is full of curious exhibits demonstrating enormous ingenuity.
Open: Monday to Saturday 09.30–13.00hrs, Monday, Wednesday, Friday 14.00 to 17.00hrs.
Closed: Sunday.

◆

MUSEO HORNE
Via dei Benci 6
(near **Santa Croce**)
This is the collection of the English art historian Herbert Percy Horne, who wrote the classic book on Botticelli in 1908 (still in print). His museum is most interesting for its Renaissance furniture; its pictures are mostly poor, though some are curious, too.
Open: 09.00 to 13.00hrs Monday to Saturday.
Closed: Sunday and holidays.

◆

MUSEO MARINO MARINI
Piazza San Pancrazio
(near **Palazzo Rucellai**, **Santa Maria Novella**)
The modern sculptor Marino Marini left a foundation from which this new museum has been formed – beautifully designed in the old church of San Pancrazio with a selection of his appealing animal or animal-like sculptures.
Open: Wednesday to Monday 10.00 to 13.00hrs, 16.00 to 19.00hrs (summer), 10.00 to 13.00 and 15.00 to 18.00hrs (winter).
Closed: Tuesday.

Local history on display at the Museo Storico Topografico

◆
MUSEO STORICO TOPOGRAFICO (MUSEUM OF LOCAL HISTORY)
Via dell'Oriuolo 4
(near the **Duomo**)
Maps, engravings and models of how Florence used to be.
Open: Monday to Wednesday and Friday to Saturday 09.00 to 14.00hrs, Sunday and holidays 08.00 to 13.00hrs.
Closed: Thursday

◆
OGNISSANTI (ALL SAINTS)
Borgo Ognissanti 42
(near **Santa Maria Novella, Santa Trinità**)
Through a passage by the church of Ognissanti is the Cenacolo del Ghirlandaio, or Ghirlandaio's refectory, where he frescoed a picture of the *Last Supper*, a traditional representation in monks' dining rooms, for obvious reasons. Also here are frescos salvaged from the rebuilt church of *St Augustine* by Botticelli and *St Jerome* by Ghirlandaio.
Open: Monday, Tuesday, Saturday 09.00 to 12.00hrs.

◆◆
ORSANMICHELE
Via dei Calzaiuoli
(near **Palazzo Vecchio, Duomo**)
This oddly named church has an odd history, half grain market and trade exchange, half shrine, or both at once: the shrine is on the ground floor, granaries used to be above. The centre of the shrine is an image of the *Madonna* by Bernardo Daddi (1347), housed in a magnificent tabernacle by Orcagna (1348–59). All around, inside and out, are images erected by the various 'trades' or guilds of Florence. Outside, in the niches belonging to the more important guilds, Nanni di Banco, Donatello and Ghiberti were encouraged to outdo one another in a series of statues breaking out of Gothic into an Early Renaissance style. The most famous of them is Donatello's *St George* (c1417), now in the **Bargello** (see page 27). The other statues still occupy their niches, new cleaned after a long campaign of restoration. Donatello's *St Mark* (far end, south side, via dei Lamberti) is epoch-making for its use of classical mannerisms, and has a dignity and authority anticipating Michelangelo. Nanni di Banco, responsible for two niches (one of four saints all together) kept up with him – and the rest tried! The bronze statues are by Ghiberti, in his own style. *Christ and St Thomas* by Verrocchio (on Via dei Calzaiuoli) was a late 15th-century replacement for Donatello's gilt-bronze *St Louis*, now in the **Santa Croce** museum (see page 49).
Open: daily 09.00 to 12.00hrs, 15.00 to 18.00hrs.

WHAT TO SEE

◆◆
OSPEDALE DEGLI INNOCENTI (FOUNDLING HOSPITAL)
Piazza della SS. Annunziata
(near **Museo Archeologico** and **Galleria dell'Accademia**)
This is *the* building with which the Renaissance style in architecture began. Built by Brunelleschi 1419–26, its frontage abandoned the current Gothic style (for which see **Orsanmichele**) and re-introduced an 'old' style, which people have since called 'classical', though it has to be said it does not look like anything Roman, Brunelleschi borrowed just as heavily from such early medieval buildings as the **Battistero**, and was concerned above all to create a 'national' or genuinely 'Florentine' style. He was very successful, and in the mid-16th century Vasari built the **Uffizi** in consciously the same style. The picture gallery in the Uffizi is poor value, but the cloisters are pretty.
Open: Monday, Tuesday, Thursday to Saturday 08.30 to 14.00hrs, Sunday and holidays 08.00 to 13.00hrs.
Closed: Wednesday.

◆◆
PALAZZO MEDICI-RICCARDI (MEDICI PALACE)
Via Cavour 1
(near **San Lorenzo**, **Cappelle Medicée**)
This is the house that Cosimo the Elder built between 1444 and 1464, deliberately conservative and traditional in its outside appearance, though the interior courtyard and the little chapel (all that survives of the Renaissance rooms) attest to a

more up-to-date taste. Originally its corners were open loggias, for public use as meeting places, but they were closed in the 16th century. In the 17th century, when the Medici dukes had long since moved out to live in the **Palazzo Vecchio** and the **Palazzo Pitti** it was bought by the Riccardi and extended by seven windows; in this part of the palace is Luca Giordano's Baroque ceiling painting glorifying the Medici (1683). The interior courtyard is decorated by curious roundels of classical scenes copied from antique gems (some of which can be seen in the **Museo Archeologico**, see page 34); originally they set off Donatello's bronze *David*, formerly installed on a pedestal here, now in the **Bargello** (see page 27). At the back is a private garden, where Donatello's *Judith* (now in the **Palazzo Vecchio**) may have been. Up one set of stairs in the Medici Chapel, where the family could pray in a kind of sumptuous heaven: the pews, marble floor and fresco decoration survive, although the altarpiece by Filippo Lippi is now in Berlin (replaced by a copy). Round the walls, painted by Fra Angelico's pupil Benozzo Gozzoli, troop the Three Kings on their way (from far right round to the left of the altar) in order to pay their respects to the Child represented in the altarpiece.
On the right wall, in the train of the Three Kings, come the Medici themselves, Cosimo looking old and his son Piero (just like his bust in the **Bargello**) looking in charge, with other

Palazzo Medici – Riccardi's elegant courtyard

retainers including the painter, Gozzoli, who has put his name on his cap. Lorenzo the Magnificent is not represented, and it is incorrect that the very young third King on a white horse is a portrait of Lorenzo as a boy.
Open: Monday, Tuesday, Thursday to Saturday 09.00 to 13.00, 15.00 to 18.00hrs; Sunday and holidays 09.00 to 13.00hrs. *Closed*: Wednesday.

◆◆
PALAZZO PITTI
Piazza de' Pitti
(near **Santo Spirito**, **Santa Maria del Carmine**)
The Pitti Palace began life in the mid-15th century as an ambitious palace designed by Brunelleschi for Luca Pitti, who wished to outdo the **Palazzo Medici**. The family subsequently fell on bad times, and the palace was bought by the Medici dukes who, via the **Uffizi** and the **Ponte Vecchio**, linked it in with their

primary residence in the **Palazzo Vecchio**; they also extended it and laid out the **Giardino di Bóboli** behind. The palace now houses a collection mostly of 16th-century pictures, and also, silverwork and jewellery (**Museo degli Argenti**); also porcelain and the Contini Bonacossi collection in the outhouses of the Gardens, (see **Giardino di Bóboli**).

The Pitti Palace gallery is a very important collection but it never has quite the same impact as the Uffizi, partly because it is badly displayed and lit and the pictures are dirtier. It is a bit of a labyrinth and the pictures are hung in an almost random order, with works by the same artist often shown in different rooms. However, most of the major masterpieces are in the front rooms, overlooking the piazza: they include Raphael's portraits of Angelo Doni and his wife and his round *Madonna della Sedia*, and works by Perugino, Fra Bartolommeo, Andrea del Sarto,

Titian, Van Dyck, Rubens, Guido Reni; there is a Filippo Lippi, a 15th-century interloper, in a back room. Some of the ceilings hae frescos in the latest baroque style of interior decoration by Pietro da Cortona and Andrea Saachi. *Open*: Tuesday to Saturday 09.00 to 14.00hrs; Sundays and holidays 09.00 to 13.00hrs. *Closed*: Monday

◆

PALAZZO RUCELLAI
Via della Vigna Nuova 18
(near **Santa Maria Novella**, **Santa Trinità**)

Giovanni Rucellai, who built the family palace and the loggia opposite, and the chapel in the church of San Pancrazio round the corner (*open*: only Saturday, 17.00 to 19.30hrs), and the façade of **Santa Maria Novella**, also left a diary accounting for it all. He was a typical Florentine merchant, but an outstanding one. For his public works, undertaken for the glory of 'himself, his family and his city', he employed Leon Battista Alberti, poet and pundit as well as architect, and they are all

Equestrian statue of Cosimo I, Medici Duke of Tuscany

unusual, experimental. In particular the Rucellai Palace is the only one amid so many (for instance the enormous Strozzi Palace, just across the Via dei Tornabuoni from the Rucellai) to feature the classical orders on its façade. It has opposite one of the few surviving private loggias – both for parties and to be a kind of park bench – in this city which in the 16th century had more than 60. Rucellai's sail emblem, to be seen on all his buildings, is a reference to the winds of Fortune – the sail is full, which means a following wind.

◆◆
PALAZZO VECCHIO
Piazza della Signoria
(near **Uffizi**, **Ponte Vecchio**)
In the 14th and 15th centuries the Palazzo Vecchio was the main government building of the Florentine republic, presiding over the central square of the city, where people still gather to voice their feelings. In those days they did it more violently, and the government might need the Palace's massive protection. The square once again inflamed passions when in the late 1980s it was excavated by archaeologists on the track of Roman Florence – a colossal expense of money and an inconvenience that many bitterly condemned. Now all is quiet, and the soul of Savonarola (see **San Marco**, page 46) no longer flutters, though it was here he organized a 'bonfire of the vanities' and a few years later was himself burnt for heresy. It is kept at bay by the splendid equestrian statue of *Duke Cosimo I* by Giambologna (1594) and Ammannati's

beautiful fountain of *Neptune* – well, the bronze nymphs are beautiful, but their marble master is almost as ugly as Bandinelli's awful *Hercules* put up to rival Michelangelo's neighbouring *David* outside the door of the Palazzo Vecchio. The *David* is now a replica; the original is in the **Galleria dell'Accademia**. The Hercules is not a replica, but looks it. Fascinating records of the debate about the original installation of the *David* survive – Leonardo, Botticelli, Ghirlandaio and other artists all put in their view. In 1540 Duke Cosimo I made the Palazzo Vecchio his residence, and its decoration inside dates almost entirely from his time (there are a few 15th-century frescos). Although much of it is dull – uninspired political allegory and history by teams of uninspired Mannerist court painters – there are some highlights, for instance in the Salone dei Cinquecento. Here in 1506 Leonardo and Michelangelo each began – but neither finished – rival frescos on opposite walls. Hope still burns of one day being able to rediscover their work beneath the present battle scenes. In one corner (not always open) the 'studiolo' of Duke Franceso I is a perfectly preserved cubby-hole/treasure trove, richly decorated with paintings and statues by Florentine Mannerists at their finest. Also in the hall is Michelangelo's *Victory*, originally a *Slave* (see **Galleria dell'Accademia**, page 33) but converted and – for once – something like finished. It was the first of a whole series of

WHAT TO SEE

Ponte Vecchio bridging the Arno

statues made by Mannerists of one figure above struggling with one below – a series capped by Giambologna's *Rape of the Sabine* in the **Loggìa dei Lanzi**, which has three figures!

In the private apartment of Eleanor of Toledo, wife of Cosimo I, the chapel by Bronzino is also an excellent Mannerist work. In other rooms

Verrocchio's bronze *putto* from the fountain in the courtyard (the replica is by the entrance) and Donatello's *Judith* are shown. Special exhibitions are also held. *Open*: Monday to Friday 09.00 to 19.00hrs; Sunday and holidays 08.00 to 13.00hrs. *Closed*: Saturday.

◆
PONTE VECCHIO

This 14th-century bridge was very avant-garde when it was built and is still unusual because of the shops that are built across it on both sides. It was probably built on Roman foundations and has withstood a lot: floods, including the terrible one of 1966; World War II – the Germans in retreat left it, though they blew up all the other bridges – and millions of tourists. Its shops are remarkably un-touristy – but expensive! Though closed to traffic, it is still the hub of the city. Along above the shops runs the dukes' escape corridor, from the **Palazzo Vecchio**, through the **Uffizi**, across past **Santa Felicità** to the **Palazzo Pitti**.

WHAT TO SEE

◆◆◆
SAN LORENZO ✓

Piazza San Lorenzo
(near **Palazzo Medici**)
San Lorenzo was the Medici
parish church, on the same
square as the **Palazzo Medici**
built by Cosimo the Elder.
Cosimo's father had begun
rebuilding it as early as 1419,
Cosimo and his heirs lavishly
adorned it, and it became their
last resting-place: Cosimo is
buried in front of the main altar
(marked only by a plaque), other
15th-century Medici are buried
in and beside the Old Sacristy.
Some of the 16th-century family
are enshrined in Michelangelo's
Medici Chapel, and the Medici
dukes are in Buontalenti's still
larger domed chapel at the east
end. (The 16th-century chapels
have a separate entrance at the
rear of the church: see **Cappelle
Medicée**, page 31.)
The church was built by
Brunelleschi, though it was not
completed before he died and,
as is obvious, it has never
received a façade. However,
Michelangelo designed one, and
a large wooden mason's model
now in the **Casa Buonarroti** was
prepared before the project was
abandoned. Inside, with its rows
of columns on arches, it was
conceived as a return to the
Early Christian style of church,
though it had to be the same size
as the much larger Gothic
churches of the day and that
meant some ingenious
modifications by Brunelleschi
(for instance the way the
columns are heightened
between the capital and the
arch). It is laid out in a plan of

equal rectangles, which in fact
are marked out on the floor by
strips of marble, and the grey
stone mouldings work to the
same effect against the white
rendering of the walls. It is a
magnificent space, though not so
grand or so thoroughly
geometrical as his later church
of **Santo Spirito** (see page 55).
Brunelleschi began with the Old
Sacristy, on the left of the
crossing, and this remains one of
the most famous statements of
his Early Renaissance principles.
All the parts are proportionate to
each other (though the precise
mathematics are not that easy to
work out). The Sacristy was
decorated by Donatello, but
there are reports that
Brunelleschi objected to
Donatello's coloured stucco
reliefs, as spoiling its purity.
Donatello also provided the
bronze doors to the two little
rooms beside the altar chamber,
with paired figures of standing
saints which another
contemporary accused of
indecent animation, like
'skirmishing fencers'.
Just beside the chapel is the
tomb of Cosimo's sons Piero and
Giovanni Medici, a wonderfully
massive object by Verrocchio,
and just by that an *Annunciation*
by Filippo Lippi typical of his
quirkiness – normally the angel
comes in on the left and the
Virgin receives on the right, but
Filippo sets up the scene with all
the latest geometric perspective,
and then plants the angel over in
the Virgin's compartment!
Just before the crossing are
Donatello's last masterpieces,
strange pulpits spilling over with
poignant and dramatic

The cloister, San Lorenzo

representations of Christ's death and Resurrection; some parts were finished after his death but his spirit pervades the whole. There is also a beautiful marble tabernacle by his pupil Desiderio da Settignano. Outside in the cloister is the entrance to Michelangelo's famous vestibule to the **Biblioteca Laurenziana** (Laurentian Library). It is a characteristic piece of self-indulgence, but this time at least the main commission, the Library, was completed: Michelangelo then designed this extraordinary vestibule as it were to take your mind off the books. Seeing is believing (and photographing in the small space is almost impossible): Michelangelo uses both classical forms and Brunelleschian grey stone against white rendering, but he turns them all topsy turvy. His superbly elegant steps are hardly the most efficient design for a man and his two servants to go up, as Michelangelo said he had in mind.

Church – *open*: 08.00 to 12.00hrs, 15.30 to 17.30hrs. Laurentian Library – *open*: Monday to Saturday 09.00 to 13.00hrs; *closed*: Sunday.

WHAT TO SEE

◆◆◆
SAN MARCO (FRA ANGELICO MUSEUM) ✓

Piazza San Marco
(near **Galleria dell'Accademia**, **Sant'Apollonia**, **Museo Archeologico**)

These Dominican monks of San Marco originally established in Fiésole, strictly upheld their rule, unlike those of **Santa Maria Novella** (see page 51). This included not owning any property. So Cosimo de' Medici bought the land and built their buildings for them, using his own architect Michelozzo. Though the church was later transformed, the conventual buildings including the cloister, the library, Cosimo's honorary cell, Fra Angelico's paintings, and the cell of the preacher Savonarola (who dominated Florence at the end of the 15th century) are all wonderfully preserved.

The first room on the right off the cloister houses a collection of Fra Angelico's altarpieces. His *Deposition* shows his vivid, clear, ultra-bright style, as pious as it is pure. A side to his painting that is more human and less angelic is that of his *predellas*, the little

Fra Angelico: faith revealed in art

panels in which episodes from the lives of the saints standing in the altarpieces were told: Fra Angelico was a master of narrative, and there are some excellent examples here. Passing the Chapter House, with a large *Crucifixion* by Angelico, you go up the stairs to the dormitory cells, most of which contain frescos by Angelico or his workshop. At the top of the stairs the *Annunciation* is difficult to miss; tucked away round to the right, past the entrance to the library, is Cosimo's cell, with an *Adoration of the Magi*. Though the windows of one side have now been blocked in, Michelozzo's library is still full of light, and has a marvellous serenity. Such serenity is lacking in the cells, where the frescos illustrate Christ's torments. Right round the corridor at the far end is Savonarola's cell: he was prior here, and he, and his particular kind of piety, were initially favoured by the Medici, whom he later helped to drive out of the city – before meeting his own death after clashing with the Pope.

Open: Tuesday to Saturday 09.00 to 14.00hrs, Sunday and holidays 09.00 to 13.00hrs.
Closed: Monday.

San Miniato, interior

◆◆◆
SAN MINIATO ✓

off Piazzale Michelangelo
San Miniato is an essential call on
any visit to Florence, not only for
the church itself, but for its view
over the city (which may also be
taken from Piazzale
Michelangelo just below it).
Especially if you are coming
from more northern climes, it is a
joy to go up the paths with their
sweet-smelling trees and shrubs
and feel the friendly warmth of
the sun on the stone balustrades
– though inside the marble-clad
church is contrastingly dark and
cool. If you visit the church shop,
do not be surprised to hear an
Irish accent as there are several
Irish monks here. The church is
late 11th-century, with marble
cladding like that of the

Looking north from San Miniato

Battistero; having been restored in the 19th century, it is more colourful and does not have that fumigated, stripped feeling of recent restorations of Romanesque churches, which is refreshing. Its most important objects, however, are Early Renaissance, in particular the Cardinal of Portugal's chapel off the middle of the nave, a collective masterpiece by the sculptor Antonio Rossellino and the painters Baldovinetti and brothers Antonio and Pietro Pollaiuolo (but his altarpiece is a copy; the original is in the **Uffizi**, see page 55), with faience ceiling by Luca della Robbia.

(The saintly Cardinal was a nephew of the king of Portugal, who paid for this monument in the city where he died in 1459.) Luca della Robbia also decorated the tabernacle in front of the steps to the crypt, housing 14th-century paintings by Taddeo Gaddi. In the upper choir, the parapet and pulpit and parts of the great mosaic are 13th-century. In the sacristy there are frescos of the *Life of St Benedict* by Spinello Aretino. *Open*: daily 08.30 to 12.00hrs, 15.00 to 18.00hrs (closing earlier in winter).

SANTA CROCE

Piazza Santa Croce
(near **Casa Buonarroti,
Bargello**)

This is the main Franciscan church in Florence, built for preaching and with a large square in front in case of overflow. The church is 14th-century, but its façade is 19th-century, the city having been successfully conned into believing that the architect (Nicolò Matas) was following an original design he had found. The church has to offer chiefly frescos by Giotto and other 14th-century artists, and tombs, some important as sculpture, some important more for their occupants – also, as soon as you enter, a beautiful *Madonna* carved by Antonio Rossellino. The first tomb on the right is Michelangelo's, designed by Vasari; opposite is Galileo's 18th-century tomb. Also on the right wall, Donatello's 'Cavalcanti' *Annunciation* is both elegant and forceful. Beside it the tomb of chancellor Leonardo Bruni by Bernardo Rossellino was one of the first 'humanist' tombs – breaking with the standard Gothic format and introducing classical architecture. Opposite, in the same mould, another by Desiderio da Settignano, with overlong garlands.

Of the east end chapels, the two to the right of the chancel are – or were – by Giotto. Both unfortunately are damaged, but some outstanding parts remain, for instance of the monk grieving over St Francis's death. Much better preserved is the one on the far left by Maso di Banco, a close follower of Giotto, with a memorable scene of Pope St Sylvester taming a pink dragon. A gate on the right of the church gives into the cloister, now the **Museo di Santa Croce**. The most important item in the museum is the Chapter House or Pazzi Chapel, a mature work by Brunelleschi. It is worked out by an exact geometry, though it is a rectangle rather than a square. Marble strips on the floor are as important as the pilasters on the walls in this graph-paper space. More obviously classical is the little portico, with a barrel vault with Roman 'coffering'.

In the former refectory Cimabue's *Crucifix*, the worst

The crucifixion, Santa Croce

victim of the 1966 flood, is housed, together with Donatello's *St Louis* (from **Orsanmichele**) and a couple of *Saints* by Domenico Veneziano. You can wander through the rest of the convent buildings into a second cloister amid more minor works of art.

Church – *open*: 07.30 to 12.30hrs, 15.00 to 18.00hrs (15.00 to 17.00hrs Sundays).

Museum – *open*: Thursday to Tuesday 10.00 to 12.30hrs, 14.30 to 18.30hrs in summer (15.00 to 17.00 in winter); *closed*: Wednesday.

Santa Croce's facelift ...

SANTA FELICITÀ
Piazza Santa Felicità
(near **Palazzo Pitti**, **Ponte Vecchio**)
Passing under the escape route which masquerades as the church's porch on its way from the **Ponte Vecchio** to the **Palazzo Pitti**, turn to the first chapel on the right, where Pontormo painted the amazing altarpiece of Christ's *Deposition* and further decoration to which the young Bronzino also contributed. The *Deposition*, in unreal colours, is a Mannerist masterpiece 1525–8.
Open: daily 08.00 to 12.00hrs and 16.00 to 18.00hrs.

◆◆◆ SANTA MARIA DEL CARMINE ✓

Piazza del Carmine
(near **Santo Spirito**, **Palazzo Pitti**)
The Carmelite friars were some of the most progressive, artistically speaking, in Early Renaissance Tuscany. The painter Fra Filippo Lippi was one of their number, till he became a little too progressive in another sense by liaising with a nun. While he was a boy he was able to witness the painting of the frescos by Masolino and Masaccio in the Brancacci Chapel of the Carmelite church in Florence. Left incomplete in 1428, they were finished by Filippo's illegitimate son Filippino Lippi in 1485. In later ages the vault of the Chapel was repainted and it suffered by fire, then in 1990 a major restoration was completed and the frescos emerged at last from beneath a grubby, waxy film to something like their original clarity.
In most places it is not difficult to distinguish the hands of Masaccio, Masolino and Filippino. The subject is the legend of St Peter. On the upper level Masolino's *Raising of Tabitha* is a disjointed, anecdotal narrative compared with the weighty drama of Masaccio's *Payment of the tribute money* opposite. Some of the finest scenes are those beside the window. On the lower register most – but not all – of the painting is by Filippino Lippi.
Brancacci Chapel – *open*: Monday to Saturday 10.00 to 17.00hrs, Sunday and holidays 13.00 to 17.00hrs. *Closed*: Tuesday.

◆◆◆ SANTA MARIA NOVELLA ✓

Piazza Santa Maria Novella
(near station, **Duomo**)
This was the main Dominican church of Florence, built during the 13th century but luxuriously adorned during the 14th and 15th centuries, while its clergy grew lax and attached to worldly ways (as opposed to the Observant or strict Dominicans of **San Marco**).
In its cloisters the protagonists of Boccaccio's *Decameron* met to decide to flee the city during the Black Death, going off to tell themselves stories while they passed the time in the safety of the country. It is a beautiful church with all its striped stonework, not too badly damaged by the 16th-century 'improvements'. Its façade was provided by Alberti with the money of Giovanni Rucellai (see **Palazzo Rucellai**, page 40), an odd combination of 'old-style' Romanesque coloured stone patterning with Brunelleschi's geometry.
The church's frescos are the finest in Florence. On the left nave wall, Masaccio's *Trinity* (1428) is his most complex work, a precocious example of Renaissance perspective, of Renaissance architecture (though only painted), of Renaissance portraiture (the donors and the poignant Virgin), of Renaissance study of the nude (Christ's body, shown strained in agony). At the east end, on the left, a marvellous glowing altarpiece of the mid-14th century by Orcagna, amid frescos otherwise difficult to see.

WHAT TO SEE

In the central chapel, pretty, charming, anecdotal frescos (and stained glass) by Ghirlandaio (late 15th-century): the scenes higher up can hardly be seen, but he knew that and delegated them to his assistants, one of whom may have been the boy Michelangelo. To its right, the Strozzi chapel, with frescos a few years later by Filippino Lippi, is colourful, dramatic, bizarre.

The Cloister (entrance to the left of the church) is known as the Chiostro Verde after the monochrome green in which it was painted. However, the Chapter House (later called the Spanish Chapel) was splendidly decorated in 1365–70 by Andrea Bonaiuto in vivid colours and epic detail: the subject is, roughly, the redemption of the human race by Christ with the aid of the Dominicans. Along the wall leading to the Chapter House, some of the frescos are by Uccello, notably his famous *Noah's Flood* (after 1447) with its extraordinary perspective. Church – *open*: 07.00 to 11.30hrs, 15.30 to 17.00hrs. Cloisters – *open*: Saturday to Thursday, 08.30 to 12.00hrs. *Closed*: Friday.

◆◆
SANT'APOLLONIA (CENACOLO DI SANT'APOLLONIA: CASTAGNO MUSEUM)
Via XXVII Aprile 1
(near **San Marco**)
There is only one room to see, the former refectory of the convent, but both the *Last Supper* by Andrea del Castagno and the more damaged

... a façade in a crowd

Resurrection above are magnificent – and a robust

antidote to his contemporary Fra
Angelico's pink piety nearby in
**San Marco (Fra Angelico
Museum)** (see page 46).

Open: Tuesday to Saturday
09.00 to 14.00hrs, Sunday and
holidays 09.00 to 13.00hrs.
Closed: Monday.

A quiet corner of Santo Spirito

◆◆
SANTA TRINITÀ
Piazza Santa Trinità
(near **Ognissanti**, **Ponte Vecchio**)
The major interest in this church is the Sassetti chapel with its frescos by Ghirlandaio, but on the way up the nave on the right observe the chapel with an altarpiece (*The Annunciation*) and frescos by Lorenzo Monaco, painted in the 1420s before the arrival of Masaccio. The Sassetti chapel, with rich classical tombs and lively frescos, is wonderfully complete, beautifully preserved since 1486; it is all very personal, with Sassetti's friends (including the Medici) shown looking on in the frescos, and with a miracle in the fresco above the altar represented as if it were happening in the street outside. Elsewhere in the church are tombs from the 15th century. *Open*: 07.00 to 12.00hrs, 16.00 to 19.00hrs, Sunday 16.00 to 17.30hrs.

◆
SANTISSIMA ANNUNZIATA
Piazza Santissima Annunziata
(near **Ospedale degli Innocenti**, **Duomo**, **San Marco**, **Galleria dell'Accademia**)
This would have been a very interesting church if it had been left as it was or was meant to be

in the 15th century – especially for its octagonal east end. As it is, the entrance 'atrium' is worth seeing for its frescos, mostly early 16th century, by Andrea del Sarto, Pontormo, Rosso Fiorentino. Inside, the shrine of the Tabernacle of the Annunziata still excites popular devotion. *Open*: 08.00 to 12.30hrs, 16.00 to 18.30hrs, Sunday 16.00 to 17.30hrs.

◆
SANTO SPIRITO
Piazza Santo Spirito
(near **Palazzo Pitti**, **Santa Maria del Carmine**)
Though fundamentally similar to his earlier church of **San Lorenzo**, Brunelleschi's Santo Spirito differs in scale – it is bigger. It is still more rigorously designed in terms of squares and cubes, generating the whole church from its modular unit almost like a computer diagram. Begun at the end of Brunelleschi's life, in 1436, it was not completed until the end of the 15th century, as is shown by the altarpieces of that date in the different family chapels round the east end. The large Baroque altar and the ceiling are not original, but do not spoil the all-important lines of the church. Unfortunately the altarpieces are poor; only the marble altarpiece by Andrea Sansovino is of top quality. However, do not miss the octagonal Sacristy and the richly 'coffered' passage added by Giuliano da Sangallo in the 1490s.
Open: daily 08.00 to 12.00hrs, 16.30 to 19.00hrs.

SPEDALE DEGLI INNOCENTI
See OSPEDALE

◆◆◆
UFFIZI ✓

Piazzale degli Uffizi
(near **Palazzo Vecchio**, **Orsanmichele**, **Ponte Vecchio**)
Everyone who comes to Florence has to go to the Uffizi, and often there is a queue to get in. Fortunately there is a café so you can take refreshment without having to go out again (there is no readmittance). To avoid the queues try coming late in the day or, failing that, at lunchtime. The Uffizi is divided into three (or four) main parts: the collection of classical sculpture, much of it given by the Pope to the Medici dukes and the original pride of the Gallery; the collection of Tuscan Renaissance paintings (up one side); the collection of paintings from other parts of Italy and dating from later than the 15th century (down the other side). The possible fourth part is the

Hopeful artists outside the Uffizi

WHAT TO SEE

drawings collection, some of which are on show half-way up the long haul upstairs to the pictures on the top floor.

The Uffizi was built for the Medici dukes by Vasari in the 16th century as offices below (hence the name) and gallery above; the system remains unchanged. Just off the ticket office, do not miss Castagno's frescos of famous men installed in a former church on the site. Upstairs, on the entrance side the Tuscan paintings are arranged chronologically, starting with three enormous *Madonnas* by Giotto, Duccio and Cimabue, the three founders of the 'first manner' (see **Background**) of painting, dating from either side of 1300. In smaller rooms follow some spectacular examples of Sienese painting, above all Simone Martini's *Annunciation* (1333) and Ambrogio Lorenzetti's *Presentation in the Temple* (1342), showing the 'state of the art' in perspective immediately after Giotto. Then comes Gentile da Fabriano's *Adoration of the Magi* (1423), a glittering *tour de force* with exquisite details. The Early Renaissance begins with Masaccio and Masolino's shared *Madonna with St Anne*, Domenico Veneziano's strangely pink and green altarpiece of *The Madonna and Four Saints*, Paolo Uccello, Fra Angelico, Piero della Francesca. There is a marvellous collection of works by Filippo Lippi, beautifully finished but always lively, too, and some vigorous works by Pollaiuolo. Now there follows another large room, dominated by the 'Portinari' altarpiece by the

Flemish artist Hugo van der Goes (but painted for the Florentine merchant family of Portinari, whose portraits appear in it) and by the works of Botticelli, including the famous *Primavera* and *Birth of Venus.* Both have recently been cleaned and Venus's long hair has turned from dull yellow to bright gold. Don't miss the vivid self-portrait by Filippino Lippi, looking as fresh as if it has been done yesterday.

Room XV contains early works by Leonardo da Vinci, including the *Baptism of Christ* by his master Verrocchio in which Leonardo painted the angel – at which, so Vasari relates, Verrocchio himself gave up painting in despair, concentrating on sculpture. From here you have to go out into the corridor in order to proceed; and there is an interruption to the chronological sequence, because of the 'tribune'. This octagonal room was originally the centrepiece of the gallery, and there is a famous picture by the English artist Zoffany showing a crowd of English lords on the Grand Tour studying the paintings and classical sculpture in it. Now it is hung mostly with portraits of the ducal family by Bronzino – hard, exact, glassy images of great fascination.

Adjoining the tribune, the next rooms show paintings by 15th-century artists of other Italian schools – for instance Mantegna of Mantua, Bellini of Venice – and by Flemish and by German artists such as Holbein and Dürer.

Across the 'bridge' on the other

side the 16th century begins, with Michelangelo's stupendous Doni' *tondo* or round painting. This has been newly cleaned and its extraordinarily rich detail is in wonderful condition. There are also Raphaels and works by Andrea del Sarto – haunting, monumental altarpieces – and by the Mannerist disciples of Michelangelo (Pontormo, Rosso Florentino). A further room has a fine collection of Venetian paintings, including Titian's *Venus of Urbino*, but these being foreigners they come last on the list for conservation and cleaning! At the end, dramatically terminating the enfilade of doors, is Parmigianino's Mannerist

masterpiece, *The Madonna with a long neck* – and just about every other element of her anatomy is also distorted for the sake of a frozen, unfeeling elegance, a fitting monument to an age of increasingly artificial convention. There follow interesting 16th-century works but few are by any great names, and in truth the collection henceforward becomes rather more random and bitty. The great age of Florentine painting you have seen, and the rest of the gallery is perhaps more for browsing.

Originally full of bureaucrats, the Uffizi is now full of art

Artists present include
Veronese, Tintoretto, Annibale
Carracci, Caravaggio, Rubens
and many more, into the 18th
century (ending with one Goya).
The Uffizi, as mentioned, was
primarily an office building and
secondly a picture gallery. It also
served for defence, providing an
escape route from the **Palazzo
Vecchio** to the river's edge and
then across the **Ponte Vecchio**
to the **Palazzo Pitti** and the
ultimate safety of the **Belvedere**
fortress.

The Uffizi's shaded colonnade

This escape corridor, also built
by Vasari, still runs across the
Ponte Vecchio and is now hung
with the ducal collection of
portraits and self-portraits. The
Uffizi end of the corridor was
bomb damaged in 1993 and
may now not be visitable (tel:
218341). Otherwise the Uffizi is
open: Tuesday to Saturday 09.00
to 19.00hrs; Sunday and holidays
09.00 to 13.00hrs.
Closed: Monday.

EXCURSIONS FROM FLORENCE

Other Towns in Tuscany

Both within the immediate vicinity of Florence and further afield there is much to see and enjoy. Tuscany has a considerable seaside (see **Children**, **Sport and Leisure**, page 104) as well as countryside. You may like to do a wine tour of the Chianti region (see **Food and Drink**, page 87). In summer it is possible to tour the villas and gardens of Tuscany (enquire at the Tourist Office or at travel agencies), and virtually all the villas of the Medici in the countryside round Florence such as **Poggio a Caiano**, **Artimino**, etc) are open to the public (details at the Tourist Office). Those interested can visit the Etruscan museums and tombs in and around Chiusi, Cortona or Volterra. Listed below are some of the most delightful towns in the region.

◆◆

AREZZO

Arezzo is a hill-top town with a pretty, oddly sloping central square, which is splendidly decorated on the first Sunday of September for the *Giostra del Saraceno* (see **Special Events**) the Saracen's Joust. (On the first weekend of other months an antique market is held there.) In the church of **San Francesco**, Arezzo has one of the most important series of paintings an art-lover will want to see, the frescos of the *Legend of the Holy Cross* by Piero della Francesca, his greatest single surviving work (about 1450–60). It has, too, other churches worth visiting,

and a decent museum.

San Francesco is in the centre of the town, at the top of the road that leads up from the station. Piero's frescos are in the chancel; there are other paintings in the church but none of great interest. According to the legend, the tree from which the wood for the Cross would be taken was growing at the time of Adam, with whom the cycle starts; also when Solomon met the Queen of Sheba. After the Crucifixion the Cross won battles for Constantine and another for the Emperor Heraclius against the Persian Khosroes (represented on the lower level on each side); also shown is St Helena having rediscovered it and sorting it out from rival crosses by having it work a miracle. The frescos have a marvellous abstract quality, though their detail is vivid.

Further up the hill, on the **Corso Italia**, the **Pieve di Santa Maria** has one of the most extravagant Romanesque façades in Tuscany, tier upon tier of colonnades – outdoing anything even in Lucca, where such façades abound. Inside, the picture on the main altar is a well preserved Pietro Lorenzetti.

Behind the Pieve, the **town square** is flanked by Gothic buildings of various kinds except for the Loggia built by Vasari about 1575. Arezzo was Vasari's native town and his house here is also preserved, **Via XX Settembre 55**: he decorated it himself and it is rather charming (*open*: Monday, Wednesday to Saturday 09.30 to 13.30hrs. Sunday and holidays 09.00 to 13.00hrs; *closed*: Tuesday).

EXCURSIONS

The poet Petrarch was also 'Aretine' (or his father was; he did not live here), and so was the chancellor and historian of Florence, Leonardo Bruni, who is buried in Santa Croce in Florence. At the bottom of Via Settembre XX is the **Museo d'Arte Medioevale e Moderno**, with medieval and Renaissance works (*open*: Tuesday to Saturday 09.30 to 15.30hrs, Sunday and holidays 09.00 to 13.00hrs; *closed*: Monday). At the top of XX Settembre, is **San Domenico**, a fine church with a crucifix said to be by Cimabue. The **Cathedral** is also attractive; up on the left by the altar is a solitary fresco of *Mary Magdalene* by Piero della Francesca, and Bishop Guido Tarlati, who died in 1330, was given shortly afterwards a magnificent tomb.

The Tourist Office is at Piazza Risorgimento 116 (tel: (0575) 20839/23952).

◆
BARGA
An unspoilt village north of Lucca with a delightful **Cathedral** and an elaborate 12th-century pulpit; there is an **opera festival** here in summer.
Enquire Tourist Office at Lucca (tel: (0583) 491205).

◆
CERTALDO
Certaldo is famous as Boccaccio's home town and for its town hall, widely reproduced on posters and one of the most picturesque in Tuscany.

◆
CORTONA
Much favoured by the English,

Cortona is a small town all of brown sandstone with a single main street. It has a splendid picture by Fra Angelico in its **Museo Diocesano** (*open*: daily 10.00 to 13.00hrs, 16.00 to 19.00hrs (summer), 15.00 to 17.00hrs (winter); *closed*: Monday) – and some by other artists. In the church of **San Domenico** there are frescos by Fra Angelico and others. From the ramparts there is a charming view, in particular on to the clear outline of its Roman amphitheatre. Cortona was also an Etruscan centre and has an Etruscan museum (**Museo dell'Accademia Etrusca**). On the way up into the town you will see two beautiful isolated churches, one of which, the earlier, the **Madonna del Calcinaio**, is by Francesco di Giorgio (1485–1513) and is also beautiful inside; the other, **Santa Maria Nuova**, is by Vasari (1554), and second best.
Tourist office: Via Nazionale 70 (tel: (0575) 63052).

◆
FIÉSOLE
There is nothing of great interest to see in Fiésole except the view over Florence from the town park. Nearby are the remains of its Roman amphitheatre. Behind the theatre is the ruin of a sophisticated bath house. At weekends in summer it may be crowded and it is also the venue for the *Fiésole Estate* or festival (see **Culture**, **Entertainment**, **Nightlife**, page 101).

◆
GALLUZZO
Just a few miles outside Florence, the **Certosa di**

Galluzzo (Galluzzo Charterhouse) was founded by Nicola Acciaiuoli, chancellor of Naples and an outstanding international politician of the 14th century. Its 16th-century

Arezzo: Pieve di Santa Maria from the Corso Italia

refurbishings include remarkable frescos by Pontormo (1522–25).

62

◆◆◆
LUCCA ✓

Lucca is a town of real character,
obtained perhaps during an
extraordinary history of
independence from greater
powers – in particular Florence –
until 1799, when it fell to
Napoleon. Enormous efforts
were made by Florence, to
capture Lucca, especially after
Pisa had fallen to her in 1406, but
all in vain. From the days when
her silk industry made her rich,
Lucca still has beautiful walls
with intact gates and bastions
built against the dukes of
Tuscany in the 16th and 17th
centuries. It rejoices also in a
number of fine Romanesque
churches, a fascinating square
still in the oval shape of the
Roman amphitheatre from which
its houses were partly built,
some outstanding works of
Renaissance art, shops with Art
Nouveau fronts, an active opera
house, the annual procession of
the *Volto Santo* (see **Special
Events**, page 106) and excellent
produce, above all olive oil,
meant to be the best in Tuscany.
The centre of the town is the
wide open **Piazza Napoleone**;
there is also a Napoleonic palace
here, where Napoleon's sister
Elisa resided. The **Cathedral** is
13th-century, with the first of
Lucca's several tiered façades. It
contains the *Volto Santo*, a
wooden statue of Christ (robed,
not naked, in the older Byzantine
tradition) that is paraded through
the city on the eve of the feast of
the Holy Cross (13 September).
It also has the beautiful tomb of
Ilaria del Carretto by Jacopo
della Quercia (c1405), an

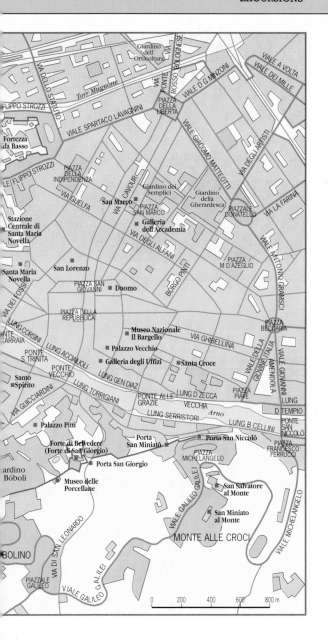

Typical of many Tuscan hill towns, Pienza is an arresting sight

Ophelia resting among dancing cupids. Other churches with similar tiered façades are **San Michele**, just by the Piazza Napoleone, and **San Frediano**, along the main **Via Fillungo**, opposite the amphitheatre/square; both also contain good-quality works of art, especially San Frediano. Walking between the two, you will pass the best shops, and both the liveliest and the oldest part of the town.

The **Museo Nazionale** in the Villa Guinigi (off to the east of the town) has both Etruscan and Roman archaeology and pictures, notably by Fra Bartolommeo. This is the superior collection, but there is another in the **Pinacoteca Nazionale** in Palazzo Mansi, Via Galli Tassi 43, at the opposite, west end of town.

Tourist Office: Piazza Guidiccioni 2 (tel: (0583) 491205).

◆◆
MONTEPULCIANO

Montepulciano is another beautiful Tuscan town on a gentle hill-top; it makes a famous wine, the 'noble wine' (*vino nobile*) of Montepulciano, and just outside its walls to the southwest it has an ideal Renaissance church, **San Biagio**, built by Antonio da Sangallo the Elder (1518–45) – ideal because perfectly symmetrical and proportionate, being built as a circle (the dome) on a square. It may be compared with the two similar churches outside Cortona and with Santa Maria dei Carceri outside Prato: all were built to house miracle-working images of the Madonna. Inside the town, the **Cathedral** is rather gloomy, but with interesting remains of a tomb by Michelozzo (1430s). But it is rewarding to walk through the town and along its ramparts, for the view and for the Gothic, Renaissance and baroque churches and palaces.

PIENZA

This untouched little town makes a memorable excursion from Siena. Pienza is named after one of the most successful 'humanists' or professional scholars and diplomats of the Early Renaissance. This minor Sienese aristocrat rejoiced in the name of Aeneas Sylvius Piccolomini until he became Pope Pius II in 1458. The papal tiara enabled him to found his family's fortune, to build this city from what had been a mere village, and to write garrulous memoirs from which Burckhardt drew plentifully when he wrote his great history of the Renaissance as the age of the individual. The story of his papacy told in pictures can be seen in the Piccolomini Chapel in Siena Cathedral.

Pienza (named after him) is more or less as Pius II built it, with a cathedral, a family palace and a bishop's palace all on the same square as he planned them and built them. The **Cathedral** is in an awkward, still half-Gothic, Early Renaissance style. The interior was influenced by churches Pius had admired during his travels in Germany. Pius relates that the architect, Bernardo Rossellino, came to him in fear and trepidation because he had grossly overspent his budget, but Pius congratulated him because he had put magnificence before thrift. It has a fine collection of matching altarpieces by Sienese painters of the time. The **Palace** is on the pattern of the Palazzo Rucellai in Florence, sited for its excellent view as Pius explains in his memoirs.

PISA

The **Camposanto** complex in Pisa is one of the most famous spaces in the world, and has many beauties besides the **Leaning Tower**. The tower was, of course, the bell-tower or *campanile* of the cathedral, one of the oldest in Tuscany and in its enormous size witness to the importance of Pisa in the 11th, 12th and 13th centuries. It was then, together with the rival maritime powers of Venice and Genoa, one of the greatest cities in Italy. Subsequently it lost out in

Sinking feeling: Pisa's Leaning Tower

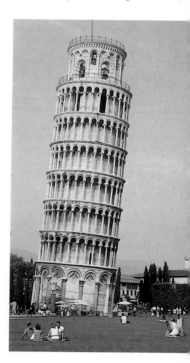

the battle for the Mediterranean and was overtaken by neighbouring Florence. It was conquered by Florence in 1406. Apart from the Camposanto complex, there is not a great deal to see in the city, excepting the Late Gothic chapel of **Santa Maria della Spina** on the banks of the River Arno, and the picture gallery of the **Museo Nazionale San Matteo**, Lungarno Mediceo (*open*: Tuesday to Saturday 08.00 to 19.30hrs, Sunday 08.30 to 13.30hrs; *closed*: Monday). This museum completes a tour of the Camposanto complex, because it contains many paintings and sculptures of the same period and by some of the same artists who worked there. It also has important fragments of a 1426 altarpiece made for the Carmelites in Pisa by Masaccio.

The Cathedral
This is the oldest part of the Camposanto complex, begun in 1065 by Buschetto who was possibly Greek; its striped patterning is probably Western, but the decoration of lozenges under blind arches may be an oriental import. It was ready to receive Bonanno da Pisa's bronze doors in 1180; unfortunately those of the front façade were lost in a 16th-century fire, though those on the side-door remain, crude but affecting. Inside it is dark and cavernous, but Giovanni Pisano's virtuoso pulpit (1302–10) can be illuminated, with its supporting statues and upper reliefs merging an energetic Gothic style with his father Nicola's solidity and firmness. The mosaics are for

the most part 13th-century. There are some 16th-century pictures, by Andrea del Sarto and Beccafumi.

The Baptistery
Next came the round Baptistery, begun in 1152, completed by Nicola and Giovanni Pisano at the end of the 13th century. Inside is Nicola's impressive pulpit (1260): it is well known that in one of the scenes the figure of the Virgin is copied from a classical sarcophagus in the Camposanto, which is significant as the kind of thing that became habitual in the later Renaissance. However, it had also occurred earlier in France (for instance at Rheims) and in southern Italy, where Nicola trained. Nicola's son, Giovanni, shows the influence of French Gothic sculpture still more clearly: his figures formerly on the outside are now kept inside round the wall.

The Leaning Tower
Last came the Leaning Tower, which was built in two stages: first from 1173, to be abandoned at the third storey when it began to lean; second in the later 13th century, after it was realised it was not going to fall down. From the joint it was built more on the vertical, but it has continued to lean. It is no longer possible to climb to the top, since its present condition has given rise to a real fear that it may yet actually fall over, even though the rate at which it has been tipping has slowed. Elaborate underpinning has been undertaken but may yet prove inadequate on this once marshy ground.

Pisa: Baptistery, Cathedral

The Camposanto ✓

Alongside the Cathedral and Baptistery the Camposanto (or cemetery) was richly decorated with frescos, including the awesome *Triumph of Death* painted in the aftermath of the Black Death (1348) by an unknown author, often thought today to have been Buffalmacco, whom Boccaccio made a prominent character in several stories in his *Decameron*. The frescos on the walls round the courtyard where the classical sarcophagi are ranged (their former occupants having been ejected to make way for the new ones) are badly faded, but the underdrawings for them can be seen in the **Museo delle Sinopie** opposite (*open*: daily 09.30 to 12.30hrs, 15.00 to 16.30hrs).

Accommodation/Restaurants
Among the hotels in Pisa, the middle-range **Hotel Mediterraneo** is recommended (Via Turati 33, tel: (050) 501133). There is no trouble finding adequate or better restaurants in the centre of town. Pisa is easily reached by rail or bus (see **Directory: Public transport**); though the station is a bit of a distance from the centre, there is a local bus in.
Tourist office: Piazza Duomo (tel: (050) 560464) or Piazza Arcivescovado (tel: (050) 560464) or at the station (tel: (050) 42291).

◆
PISTÓIA
Pistóia is not an especially attractive town, but it contains an important pulpit by Giovanni Pisano which *aficionados* will not want to miss, also Early Renaissance works in its **Cathedral**. Its **Ospedale del Ceppo** displays the most ambitious work in coloured Della Robbia faience in Italy: the *Seven Works of Mercy* made by Andrea della Robbia in the early 16th century. Otherwise the town is best known for having given its name to the pistol. Giovanni Pisano's pulpit, his most vigorous work (it has a famous scene of the *Massacre of the Innocents*), is in the church of **Sant'Andrea**. Other, contemporary pulpits are in the churches of **San Giovanni Fuorcivitas** and **San Bartolomeo** in Pantano.

Tourist Office: Via Gramsci 110 (tel: (0573) 34326).

◆
PRATO
Prato is a town that has been transformed by modern industry: it is full of traffic jams and immigrant workers from the South. In a kind of enclave in its centre stands its attractive **Cathedral**, with precious frescos inside by Filippo Lippi. It also has an imposing 13th-century **castle**, built by the emperor Frederick II, and close by a beautiful example of those square churches for miracle-working images of the Madonna (compare Cortona and Montepulciano).
This church, **Santa Maria delle Carceri**, was designed in 1485 by Giuliano da Sangallo, who finished off Brunelleschi's church of Santo Spirito in Florence and built here in very much the same style. He was recommended by Lorenzo de' Medici, whom the people of Prato consulted as the best man to know.
The Romanesque cathedral has on its right-hand corner a circular outside pulpit by Donatello: it is very like Luca della Robbia's Singing Gallery in the Museo dell'Opera del Duomo in Florence and seems to incorporate Donatello's first thoughts before he came up with his own extraordinary creation opposite in the same museum. The original panels are now in the Cathedral Museum in the **Bishop's Palace** (*open*: daily 09.30 to 12.30hrs, 15.00 to 16.30hrs, Sunday 09.30 to 12.30hrs). The pulpit was used not only for preaching but also

or displaying the relic of the Virgin's girdle which is kept in the church (still displayed on the holiest days of the year). The story of the girdle is told in fresco in the chancel of the church by Agnolo Gaddi, but far more interesting are Filippo Lippi's frescos (1460s) of the stories of SS John the Baptist and Stephen – the *Dance of Salome* (dressed like a classical nymph)

is justly famous. Also the awkward frescos attributed to Paolo Uccello in the chapel on the right of the altar should be seen. Not far from the Cathedral is the house of Francesco Datini (corner of Via Rinaldesca with Via Ser Lapo Mazzei), whose 14th-century diaries have been published under the title

Prato Cathedral, pulpit and tower

The Merchant of Prato.
Tourist Office: Via Muzzi 51 (tel: (0574) 35141).

◆◆
SAN GIMIGNANO

San Gimignano is renowned for its 13 tall towers. Once every free town in Italy had towers like San Gimignano's, built not simply as places of refuge when rival mobs ranged the streets, but also one to outdo the other. However, most towns eventually introduced laws to have them demolished, since they encouraged civil strife. Today, San Gimignano's 13 surviving private towers are outdone only by Pavia in Lombardy, but Pavia, a much larger town on the flat, cannot offer such a skyline when you approach it. San Gimignano also has some fine frescos in its churches and is a wine centre. The town centre is pedestrianised and full of cafés, *enoteche* or wine-shops and eating places. You can also walk the **ramparts**. The main church to be seen is the **Collegiata**, with an amazing square footage of frescos of the 14th century by Bartolo da Fredi and 'Barna da Siena' – whoever exactly he may have been. In a chapel in mid-nave, frescos (1475) by Ghirlandaio adorn the shrine of the local child-saint, St Fina (note the view of the town he includes in one). In the **Palazzo del Popolo** there is a gallery of 13th to 15th-century paintings of the Sienese school. More frescos, by Gozzoli (more famous for his frescos in the Medici Palace chapel in Florence), can be seen in **Sant'Agostino**.
Tourist Office: Piazza Duomo (tel: (0577) 940008).

One of San Gimignano's food stops

◆
SANSEPOLCRO

A sleepy town kept awake chiefly by its pasta factories, Sansepolcro or Borgo San Sepolcro is also the birthplace of Piero della Francesca, and its **Museo Civico** houses some stupendous examples of his work. As you go through, you see the outraged remains of a polyptych with its central panel missing: the missing panel is the *Baptism of Christ* by Piero now in the National Gallery, London. But the museum holds all the parts of Piero's altarpiece of the *Madonna of Mercy* (majestically embracing in her cloak kneeling townsfolk), and has attached to its wall his famous *Resurrection*, which was once the equivalent of the town flag (Sansepolcro means Holy Sepulchre). (*Open*: daily 09.30 to 13.00hrs, 14.30 to 18.00hrs.) Piero *aficionados* also like to visit the *Madonna del Parto* or Pregnant Madonna in a chapel near Monterchi, 11 miles (18km) to the south (well signposted).

SIENA

It was a great moment for the Sienese in 1260 when the city defeated Florence in the battle of Montaperti, but it was one of few. Mostly Siena was the underdog to her more powerful and successful neighbour on the Arno: Ghibeline when the tide of history favoured the Guelfs (see **Background**, page 7), she controlled a smaller territory and never achieved the banking and trading success of the Florentines. And the heyday of Siena was much shorter, lasting only from the mid-13th to the mid-14th century, when the Black Death extinguished her ambitions. A visible sign of the city's final relegation from the first league of Italian power is the roofless outline of an enormous extension to the **Cathedral** begun in 1339 but abandoned in 1348. Florence's successfully completed larger dome stands in eloquent contrast.

The great charm of Siena today is precisely that it is a medieval city, and the narrow streets that descend to its famous auditorium-like **Campo** are impenetrable to cars. It is a living relic of the late Middle Ages, brought even more dramatically to life on the days immediately before and on 2 July and 16 August, when the famous *Palio* or horse-race in period costume is run, not just as a pageant but still with all the passion and fervour of a football game, by Sienese from rival districts of the city.

In the years between 1260 and 1348, a few Sienese artists created works of such entrancing beauty that they influenced all Europe. While the Florentine Giotto was pressing out his solid, sculptural figures, the Sienese Duccio (active between 1278 and 1318) was refining what seems perhaps a more old-fashioned art, though it was in fact equally new and original. Duccio and his pupils Simone Martini (died 1344) and the brothers Ambrogio and Pietro Lorenzetti (both died 1348) were masters of rich, soft, delicate colours, imparting their figures with a remote, fairytale grace. The Sienese 'school' was perhaps even more important for the art of Italy and France in the second half of the 14th century than was the Florentine. It also continued very charmingly into the 15th century with such artists as Giovanni da Paolo, 1403–1482. Siena's saints also have to be mentioned. St Catherine of Siena in the later 14th century and St Bernardino in the 15th earned a national reputation for holiness – St Catherine telling the Pope what to do and San Bernardino as one of the most effective preachers of all time. He was also behind the world's oldest surviving bank, the Monte dei Paschi di Siena, originally a savings bank for dowries. However, that is all Siena. It is a bit on a mono-culture compared to the variety and bustle of Florence. If you go there on a cold day in spring you may be horrified at the bone-biting power of the wind tearing along its stone alleyways, which then begin to look rather bleak. It does not have the shops and workshops of Florence, and none of those crowded, noisy restaurants – most of the life its visitors bring with them! Nobody should miss Siena, and it is not easy to fit all the sights into a single day-trip, but a fortnight there would definitely be too long. Unless you used Siena as a base to explore the surrounding countryside – there are some beautiful places in the province of Siena (for instance, San Gimignano, Montepulciano). Tourist Office: Via di Citta 43 (tel: (0577) 280606).

Palazzo Pubblico ✓

The **Torre del Mangia** rises tall and slender high above the **Campo** and out of all proportion or relation to the main building of the **Palazzo Pubblico** beside it. A bit of Early Renaissance (1460s) sculpture clings rather uncertainly to its base. 'Public palace' is a suitably vague term to embrace the variety of governments that have occupied it during its history. It contains several rooms of frescos, two of them being world famous. One of these has on opposite walls frescos by Simone Martini of the Madonna as patroness of Siena and of the captain Guidoriccio, riding across the fought-over landscape – but new investigations of the fresco have raised doubts about its true date and whether it does not replace an earlier fresco that was really Guidoriccio. However, this would be a copy of the older one, so the argument is a bit like the question whether Homer was Homer or another man with the same name. Next door are Ambrogio Lorenzetti's frescos of *Good* and *Bad Government*, of

which especially the picture of the town and countryside under Good Government is famous. Also the allegorical figures survive, and beneath them the citizens queue, bound by the rope on which they are all to pull together in civic harmony. The corresponding pictures of Bad Government, or civil strife, are largely lost. Other rooms contain frescos by artists including Taddeo di Bartolo and Spinello

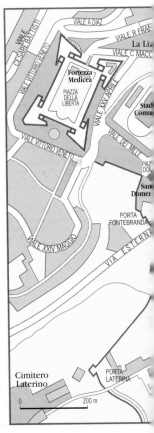

Aretino (the sea battles). On the top floor, the remains of Jacopo della Quercia's original *Fonte Gaia*, of which a replica occupies the Campo. It is very badly damaged and its high quality difficult to make out.

Cathedral

From the Campo you have a choice of which hill to climb. Having made your way up to the Cathedral, also the **Baptistery**, the **Museo dell'Opera del Duomo** and the **Ospedale di Santa Maria della Scala**, you can continue on the level for the **Pinacoteca**. Everything is well signposted. The Cathedral as it stands is a building of the late 12th century largely completed in the early 14th century, when Giovanni Pisano designed its façade and adorned it with statues now on the ground floor of the Museo dell'Opera del

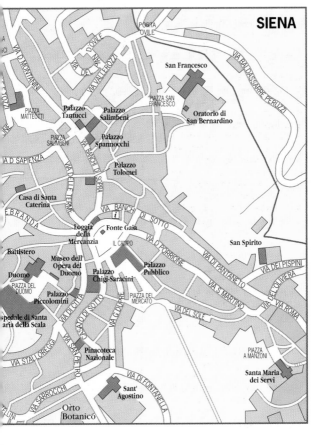

EXCURSIONS

Duomo. In 1339 there was an idea to use the existing Cathedral as the transept of a still larger one (as it were swivelling it on its dome, the predecessor that Florence Cathedral dome outswells by far). In 1348 the Black Death struck and eventually the project was abandoned, leaving the skeleton still to be seen. Once on the main altar was Duccio's *Maestà* or Virgin in Majesty, now housed in the Museo dell'Opera del Duomo, those parts of it that were not lost or scattered to museums of the world when the altarpiece was vandalously dismembered at the end of the 18th century. In its darkened chamber it is still a unique, enchanting experience. A *Madonna* by Jacopo della

Quercia on the ground floor should not be missed, and there are other good pictures upstairs. The museum is *open*: 09.00 to 13.00hrs (winter) 09.00 to 19.50hrs (summer).

Inside the Cathedral, Nicola Pisano's richly decorated pulpit (1268) occupies pride of place almost beneath the dome. The amazing picture-book marble floor is for the most part covered up for its protection, giving only glimpses of odd figures. On the left of the nave the Piccolomini altar is famous for the four statues it includes by the young Michelangelo (1501–04). Just by it is the **Piccolomini Library** (*open*: daily 10.00 to 13.00hrs, 14.30 to 17.00hrs; 19.30 summer), with a series of enormous frescos by Pinturicchio

White Duomo arising from Burnt Siena

Baptistery
In the Baptistery beneath the east end of the Cathedral the font is an unparalleled masterpiece. It was a joint work by Ghiberti, Donatello, Jacopo della Quercia and others, incorporating two panels by Ghiberti (facing the door and next to the right), one by Donatello (next to the right again), the rest by followers trying desperately to keep up. Donatello also provided some of the surrounding angels and Jacopo della Quercia designed the upper part.

Pinacoteca
The Gallery in Siena (Via San Pietro 29) has a wonderful collection of paintings, though they are all Sienese and all religious – half of them Madonnas. All the important names are there, including Duccio, Simone Martini, the Lorenzettis, Giovanni di Paolo and the 16th-century Beccafumi.
Open: Tuesday to Saturday 08.30 to 19.00hrs, Sunday 08.30 to 13.00hrs.
Closed: Monday.

Churches
Of the other directions to be taken from the Campo, you might best go behind the Palazzo Pubblico towards **Santa Maria dei Servi**, which has an early painting by Coppo di Marcovaldo (1261; right of nave) and another by Lippo Memmi (left transept). Other churches have less to see; **San Francesco**, however, has amazing angels in relief by Agostino di Duccio on the façade of the Oratory of San Bernardino. The pious may also visit the house of **St Catherine of Siena**, just below San Domenico.

telling the story of Pius II's papacy (for the Sienese Pope Pius II, see also **Pienza**). In the left transept, in the chapel of St John, the bronze *St John the Baptist* is by Donatello. Other important works of art adorn the Cathedral, the latest of them the Chigi Chapel designed by Bernini (1661).
Opposite the Cathedral the hospital of **Santa Maria della Scala** is one of the oldest still functioning in the world; it has accumulated a collection of gifts dating from the 13th century, and its central rooms are lavishly adorned with early 15th-century frescos (sometimes visitable on request in the mornings).

Accommodation

Most hotels in Siena enjoy a pleasant view over the city or landscape. Recommended are the **Duomo**, Via Stalloreggi 38 (tel: (0577) 289088) or, in a lower category, the **Cannon d'Oro**, Via Montanini 28 (tel: (0577) 44321). There are several others at all prices, and a hotel cooperative that will find you one when you arrive at San Domenico (by the bus station). The youth hostel, **Guido Riccio**, is in Via Fiorentina (tel: (0577) 52212).

Restaurants

Siena seems to have more bars than restaurants; several offer a mouthwatering array of cakes besides the Sienese speciality of *panforte*. Its best range of places to eat a meal, from plain *pizzeria* to more pretentious and expensive restaurants, is to be found round the fringe of the Campo, or also behind the Palazzo Pubblico (for example **Osteria Le Logge** in Via del Porrione 3 (tel: (0577) 48013). Set conveniently by the slope down to the Baptistery at the east end of the Cathedral is **Tre Campane**, Via delle Campane 6 (tel: (0577) 284039) offering good, straightforward Tuscan fare.

Another good *trattoria* is **Il Biondo**, Via Rustichetto 10 (tel: (0577) 280739) or **Da Vasco**, Via del Capitano 6 (tel: (0577) 288094). Smarter places include **Al Marsili**, Via del Castoro 3 (tel: (0577) 47154), featuring the best local wines. Somewhat outside the centre, the **Bottega Nova**, Strada Chiantigiana 29 (tel: (0577) 284230) is recommended. The **Enoteca Italica Permanente** in the **Fortezza Medicea** is a pleasant place to sample the best of Tuscan wine on a sunny evening or, if you wish, the right place to go into the matter very seriously! It houses the **National Wine Library**, appointments only.

Events

To book a place to watch the famous *Palio* (see above and **Special Events**) contact the Tourist Office (tel: (0577) 280551). Note that there are rehearsals in the days immediately before 2 July and 16 August that are almost as good fun.

◆

VOLTERRA

Though Volterra is well within Tuscany, its atmosphere is unlike any Tuscan town and it seems to have more in common with Lazio to the south. It is a bleak place when empty and if the weather turns. Visitors will be interested primarily either in its Etruscan past shown in the **Museo Etrusco Guarnacci**, Via Don Minzoni 15, or in the medieval and Renaissance heritage of its **Cathedral**, **Baptistery** and **Museo Civico** on Via Sarti. Tourist Office: Piazza dei Priori (tel: (0588) 86150).

Siena's Palazzo Pubblico and Campo

PEACE AND QUIET

Countryside and Wildlife in Florence and Tuscany
by Paul Sterry

At least part of the beauty of Florence lies in its setting among the rolling Tuscan hills, with their abundance of trees and shrubs. The Tuscan countryside is ideal for peaceful walks and acts as a perfect foil to the aesthetic delights of the city.

As a region Tuscany is far from uniform. It is flanked on one side by the hills and mountains of the Apennines, while to the west lies the so-called Tuscan Riviera. Although there are still areas of unspoilt natural landscape, much of the rolling countryside around Florence is actively farmed. However, the olive groves, small fields and agricultural landscape seem to harmonise perfectly with the timeless and unspoilt feel of the city. Together they create the spirit of Tuscany.

Peace and Quiet in Florence

There are so many cultural, historical and architectural sights in Florence that visitors are sometimes left overwhelmed. Fortunately, there are also numerous parks and gardens – havens of comparative peace and tranquillity – where you can sit and contemplate the city's treasures. A few of the more interesting locations are as follows:

The Cascine Park stretches along the northern shores of the River Arno and contains, among other things, a racecourse. There are two sections, one sandwiched between Viale Giorgio Washington and Viale dell'Aeronautica, and the other between Viale Abramo Lincoln and Viale degli Olmi. Birdwatchers may find something of interest in spring and cicadas serenade the summer air.

The Giardino dei Semplici, or botanic garden, is part of the Institute of Botany and lies on Via Alfonso Lamarmora south of the Piazza della Libertà. The gardens, which house many orchids, are open in the mornings only on Monday, Wednesday and Friday.

The Giardino di Bóboli lies close to the Palazzo Pitti south of the Via Romana and Via Guicciardini; there is parking off the Piazzale di Porta Romana. The terraced gardens are formal in appearance but attract butterflies and other insects, while the trees and shrubs harbour birds. The gardens are very large and are ideal for long walks.

Swifts
One of the most characteristic sound of towns and cities in Tuscany is that of screaming swifts. These aerobatic birds visit the region from May until August and parties of several dozen can be seen sweeping through the skies in search of insects. Swifts are all-black birds whose wings have a horseshoe-shaped appearance in flight. So well adapted to life on the wing are they that their legs and feet are reduced and they can do little more than shuffle along on the ground. Swifts nest in roofs and under eaves in old buildings and good sites are traditionally used year after year.

PEACE AND QUIET

The Strawberry Tree
So-called because of the resemblance of its rough textured fruit to the strawberry, the strawberry tree may grow to a height of 25 feet (8m). It is one of the most characteristic shrubs of the Mediterranean coast. The white, pendulous flowers appear from October until April and are attractive to insects. The fruits are used to make liqueurs in Italy.

The Habitats
The Tuscan countryside has a wide variety of habitats, from hill and mountains to agricultural fields, and from freshwater to the coastal environment. Each has its own characteristic wildlife which are summarised as follows:

Wildlife of the coast
Many parts of the coastline are rugged and dramatic. From the shore look for herring gulls: large, grey-winged birds with yellow legs. In the winter months, they are joined by lesser black-backed gulls, which are similar in size but have wings that are almost black. During periods of onshore winds, Cory's shearwaters sometimes appear. These brown birds fly on slender, stiffly-held wings and characteristically bank from side to side, making the most from the sea breezes.

Parts of the coast are fringed by the *macchia* vegetation so typical of the Mediterranean. This fragrant habitat is full of plants such as rosemary, thyme, tree heather and sage, and harbours birds such as the Sardinian warbler, which has mainly grey plumage, a black hood and a bright eye-ring.

Wildlife of open country and agricultural land
The verdant countryside of Tuscany is memorable and distinctive. Tall funereal cypress trees grow alongside plane trees and olive groves under which colourful flowers appear in the spring.

Birdlife includes several species of warblers and shrikes, most noticeably the red-backed shrike. This elegant little bird has a chestnut back and wings, a grey head and rump and a black mask. Its most distinctive characteristic is that it regularly impales its prey – insects and small lizards – on thorns, partly as a 'larder' but more

Green Lizard
The green lizard is the most elegant of mainland Italy's three species of true lizard; the other two are the common wall lizard and the Italian wall lizard. Males are usually entirely green and may reach a length of 14 inches (35cm), two-thirds of which is tail. The body is covered in fine black dots and mature males have a deep blue throat. Females are paler green in colour and often have two white stripes down their backs; young males may also share this characteristic. Green lizards sunbathe in the mornings and so are often found on south and east-facing hillsides. However, they are extremely wary and never venture far from the cover of stones or dense undergrowth. At the slightest sign of danger they bolt for safety. Their diet comprises mainly insects, such as crickets and grasshoppers, although they will sometimes take eggs or fruit.

Rolling Tuscan farmland

importantly so that it can be
dismembered.

Wildlife of Freshwater Habitats

Freshwater habitats are
comparatively few and far
between in Tuscany. The River
Arno, which runs through the
heart of Florence, is the largest
river in the region. Together with
its tributaries, it acts as a magnet
for many birds from the
surrounding land. In particular,
look for swallows and martins.
Swallows catch insects low over
the water and can be recognised
by their dark upperparts, white
underparts, red throat and long,
forked tail. They often mix with
sand martins – brown
upperparts, white underparts

and a brown collar – and house
martins – dark upperparts and
white underparts and rump. One
of the largest bodies of
freshwater in the region is Lago
Trasimeno, to the west of
Perúgia. Look for ducks and
waders during migration times
and warblers and grebes in the
spring and summer. Great reed
warblers are perhaps the
noisiest breeding bird around
the lake. They nest in the
reedbeds and their loud song –
reminiscent of a croaking frog –
is sung from a prominent perch.

Wildlife of the Hills and Mountains

Tuscany's rolling hills give way
eventually to the mountains of the
Apennines. Much of the lower

PEACE AND QUIET

regions have lost their original forest cover, having been cleared for agriculture. However, there are still pockets of beech woodland scattered throughout which repay investigation. Although not renowned for their ground flora, beech woods are often good for orchids in spring and summer; in the autumn, visitors should also look for fungi, many of which are edible and delicious. Woodland mammals such as martens, squirrels and edible dormice, although present, can be difficult to spot. The birdlife, however, is more visible: look and listen for warblers, finches and flycatchers. Collared flycatchers occur and can be recognised by their black-and-white plumage – they also have a white 'collar' – and their habit of catching insects from prominent perches. Where they are not wooded, hill sides are often cloaked in scrubby vegetation, a favoured habitat for lizards and snakes. These reptiles sunbathe in the open but keep a wary eye open for birds of prey circling overhead. Look for short-toed eagles – very pale, rounded wings and a barred tail – which specialise in catching snakes, and red kites, recognised by their long, reddish wings and deeply forked tail.

Almost anywhere in the Tuscan hills that looks undisturbed can be good for wildlife, but the following areas may be particularly rewarding for visitors:

Riserva Naturale Vallombrosa, east of Florence. Take route 67 to Pontassieve and then turn off to Pélago. A road winds through the hills to Tosi and Vallombrosa.

The bee-eater is one of Tuscany's most extravagant summer visitors

Orphean Warbler

Orphean warblers are among the commonest of the warblers to visit northern Italy in spring and summer. They live in open woodland and can be recognised by their grey-brown plumage, dark cap, white throat and conspicuous white eye. Although only 6 inches (15cm) long, Orphean warblers have a loud song which sounds rather like a thrush. They make a compact, woven nest in the dense undergrowth and generally rear three or four young.

Bee-eater

The bee-eater is undoubtedly the most colourful summer visitor to Tuscany – the plumage comprises a mixture of orange, yellow, green and blue – and its liquid, bubbling calls are a familiar sound over the open hillsides. As its name suggests, this bright bird feeds on insects which are caught on the wing. Bee-eaters glide through the air – the silhouette, with pointed wings and long tail with pointed central streamers, makes it easy to identify. The long, thin bill enables them to tackle stinging insects such as bees and wasps.

Riserva Naturale Camáldoli lies further to the east. Drive to Pontassieve and turn off on route 70. Then turn off to Pratovecchio and continue into the hills until you reach Eremo di Camáldoli. Near by is the **Riserva Naturale Badia Prataglia**, which can be reached either from Camáldoli or by driving north from Bibbiena as far as Badia Prataglia. From Bibbiena it is also worth exploring the hills to the south and west. For example,

take the road which leads to Castel Focognano and on to San Clemente in Valle.

Spring Flowers

One of the delights of a springtime visit to Florence and Tuscany is the sight of the wild flowers that grow everywhere. Many of the species which are so abundant there – poppies, marigolds, mayweeds and thistles– would be considered 'weeds' elsewhere, but here they thrive alongside the comparatively non-intensive agriculture. The reason that most flowers appear in the spring is related to the climate of the region. Although modified by the effect of hills, it is mainly Mediterranean in nature, with dry, hot summers and mild, wet winters. Many plants die back in the summer and begin growing again after the first autumn rains. Late winter and early spring is the optimum season for flowering, and from late February until May a succession of attractive flowers appear.

Bird Migration

Many of the birds found in Tuscany only spend the summer months on their breeding grounds, flying south in autumn to spend the winter in Africa, where the climate and feeding is better. April and May sees the arrival in Italy of these migrants, some staying to nest but more passing through on journeys northwards. Hills and mountains are good places to observe the movements of birds of prey and other daytime migrants such as swallows. The coast is good for waders and terns and many of the nocturnal migrants, such as

warblers, follow the coast and
feed in the day close to the shore.

Places to Visit in Tuscany

Although it is generally
rewarding to explore almost
anywhere in the Tuscan
countryside for interesting
wildlife, there are a few locations
that are particularly good. Details
of some of the more interesting
sites or areas are as follows:

The Arno Valley

Although not especially rich in
wildlife, a trip down the Arno
Valley from Florence to Pisa
takes in landscapes and views
which are quintessentially
Tuscan. There are rolling hills,
warm brown soils contrasting
with olives and cypress trees, as
well as the river itself. The route
passes through the towns of
Empoli, San Miniato, Pontedera
and Cáscina: explore minor
roads up into the hills for peace
and quiet.

The Apuan Alps

The Apuan Alps stretch inland
from the Tuscan coast and
provide a welcome relief from
the heat in the summer months.
Seravezza makes a good base
from which to explore the area:
drive the winding roads to
Stazzema or to Castelnuovo di
Garfagnana.

Rifugio Faunistico di Bólgheri (Bolgheri Wildlife Refuge)

The reserve lies on the Tuscan
coast between Cécina and San
Vincenzo and can be reached by
driving south from Livorno on the
E80 until the turning to Bólgheri.
Now controlled by the Italian
branch of the World Wide Fund
for Nature, access to the reserve

is only during the winter months
and by prior arrangement with
the WWF Italia, Delagazione per
la Toscana, Via San Gallo 32,
50129 Florence; there is a
walkway and an observation
tower. However, parts of the area
can be viewed from the main
road and from a minor road
which runs along the southern
boundary of the reserve to Il
Palone. Although many species
of birds breed in Bólgheri, the
greatest variety of wildfowl and
waders is seen during the winter
and during migration. The
mammals of the reserve include
wild boar, roe deer and
porcupine.

Parco Naturale della Maremma (Maremma Regional Park)

This large park lies on the coast

Olives: favourites on Italian menus

southwest of Grosseto. Open on Saturday, Sunday, Wednesday and public holidays, the number of visitors permitted each day is restricted by the sale of limited numbers of tickets available from the park office at Alberese (a short distance from the main E80) or the local post office. Within the park the landscape is unspoilt, with forests, *macchia* vegetation, wet meadows and drainage canals. The lack of hunting and disturbance has ensured a healthy mammal population including crested porcupines, wild boar, fallow deer and wild cats. Orchids are abundant in the spring under the canopy of the open pine woodland, which also serve as nesting sites for the region's birds of prey.

Hermann's Tortoise
Widespread along the Tuscan coast, Hermann's tortoises are also found some way inland as well. Rustling sounds often give them away as they trundle through the vegetation. They are found in a variety of habitats, from sand dunes to meadows and dense scrub. Tortoises feed mainly on plants, although they occasionally take carrion or slow-moving insects and molluscs. Females lay a clutch of up to a dozen hard-shelled eggs in the soil. These may take several weeks to hatch, depending on how warm the air is.

PEACE AND QUIET

A singing great reed warbler, well placed for the high notes

Riserva Naturale d'Orbetello (Orbetello Nature Reserve)

A series of lagoons, themselves part of the larger Laguna de Orbetello on the Tuscan coast south of Grosseto, make up this reserve. In addition to the tidal lagoons, there is *macchia* scrub, meadows, sand dunes and woodland. Public access is from October until April on Thursdays and Sundays; there are two visiting times each day – 10.00 and 13.00hrs – each lasting two hours in the company of a warden. There is an information centre south of Albinia and within the reserve there is a hide and an observation tower.

Further details about the reserve can be obtained from the WWF in Florence (Via San Gallo 32). Do not worry if you cannot visit the reserve, because many of the waders, ducks, terns and gulls that visit the area, either in the winter or on migration, can be seen from the three roads which run along the *tombolos* connecting Monte Argentario to the mainland. There is a scenic coastal drive if you leave the E80 at Albinia and take the coast road around the cliffs of Monte Argentario and back to the mainland along the Tombolo di Feniglia. Here visitors can see an example of re-afforestation of Mediterranean stone pines on the **Riserva Forestale Duna Feniglia** where the trees have stabilised the shifting sands.

Rifugio Faunistico Lago di Burano (Lago di Burano Wildlife Refuge)

The refuge lies a short distance to the southwest from Orbetello and is close to the E80 road.

Within the site there is a nature trail and a hide; access is on Thursdays and Sundays from September until May at 10.00 and 13.00hrs from Capabio Station. More details about the refuge can be obtained from the WWF in Florence. Waterbirds are attracted in the winter and during migration times and because hunting is not permitted animals such as foxes, roe deer and porcupines thrive.

Riserva Naturale Orrido di Botri (Orrido di Botri Nature Reserve)

Orrido di Botri lies to the northwest of Florence in the Apennine hills. It can be reached by taking the E74 to Lucca. From there, drive north on route 12 and at Borgo a Mozzano take the winding mountain road which heads northeast through Teréglio. A few kilometres beyond this village the road passes through the nature reserve. At the heart of the reserve is a deep limestone gorge. Orchids can be seen

Crested Porcupine

One of Italy's most unusual and distinctive mammals, the crested porcupine's large size and coat of spines make it unmistakable. It is probably not native to Italy but was introduced by the Romans from Africa. However, nowadays it is relatively common on hilly slopes with plenty of cover. Porcupines are generally nocturnal creatures; they are occasionally seen during the day, although usually in the vicinity of their hole. If alarmed, they shake their spines and tail – quite enough to deter almost all potential predators; this action is accompanied by loud grunts. The back is covered in a mixture of both long and short spines and these continue down the tail. Despite their superficial resemblance to hedgehogs, porcupines are in fact rodents and relatives of rats and mice.

growing beside the road in the spring. Look out for groups of crag martins which are uniform brown relatives of swallows.

Crested porcupine

PEACE AND QUIET

Golden Eagle

Golden eagles are among the most exciting birds to be seen in the hills and mountains of Tuscany, and Orrido di Botri often yields sightings. They have a wingspan of nearly 90 inches (230cm); the wings are broad and long and the separate feathers at the wing tips are easily visible. Although they do take live quarry, golden eagles will also feed on carrion. They soar effortlessly for hours, scanning the ground below for a meal.

Golden eagles nest on inaccessible rock ledges high in the mountains and raise one, sometimes two, young each year; the nest sites are traditional and occupied by the same pair year after year.

They fly close to the rock face catching insects on the wing. Blue rock thrushes can also be seen and heard at Orrido di Botri. The loud, musical song is delivered from a rocky promontory or sometimes in flight. Males have deep blue plumage while females are speckled brown.

Riserva Naturale Pania di Corfino (Pania di Corfino Nature Reserve)

Pania di Corfino lies in the Tuscan hills north of Lucca at an altitude of around 3,000 feet (900m). To reach the area, drive north from Lucca on route 12 and turn off on the 445, which heads northwest. At Castelnuovo di Garfagnana take the minor road to Corfino.

The limestone landscape here is rich in orchids and many other colourful flowers in the spring. Deer have been introduced and are encouraged in the area. Visitors should look for black-eared wheatears in this rugged landscape. Males have fawn coloured plumage with striking black wings and tail. In some forms the face and throat are also black, while in others the black is restricted to a 'mask' through the eyes. Black-eared wheatears often perch on prominent rocks and in flight show a conspicuous white rump.

Other Nature Reserves in Tuscany

In addition to those nature reserves and parks already mentioned, there are several others in the hills surrounding Florence; the countryside that comprises them is unspoilt and wildlife flourishes. The following sites are worth visiting: **Riserva naturale Acquerino**, northwest of Florence, reached by taking the minor road from Pistóia through Candeglia and on to Acquerino. The road between this village and Monachino passes through the reserve. There are three reserves in the extreme north of Tuscany. They are **Riservas naturale Piano degli Ontani, Campolino and Abetone** which lie close to one another to the northwest of Pistóia. From San Marcello Pistoiese follow route 12 northwards and turn off on the minor road to Piano degli Ontani which runs through the reserve of the same name and Campolino. This minor road eventually rejoins the main road near Abetone.

This is a mountainous region and these reserves are very close to Mount Cimone, the highest peak in the Apennines.

FOOD AND DRINK

Tuscan food has always been excellent, and it still is, thank goodness. Even in the most obvious restaurants and cafés on the most obvious tourist routes in Florence you will be given something tasty and real, whereas in the equivalent places in the centre of a hundred other cities you would be 'ripped off'. At the same time Italian food is the most user-friendly in the world ('fast food' is, after all, an Italian invention), and it is a difficult child who will not be happy with a pizza. You can eat just as well whether you want a sandwich on the hop, to cook for yourself, to buy a picnic, or take your wallet out for something substantial.

Tuscan cuisine acquired special favour in the 1980s in the inevitable reaction to *cuisine minceur*: traditional Tuscan cooking is in fact a perfect *cuisine gourmande*. It is part of the Italian genius that it can be called 'traditional' whereas in fact it has evolved constantly over the years. For instance the tomato, now almost synonymous with Italian food, is said hardly to have been used in Central Italy before the 19th century. Tuscan cooking has enjoyed much favour among the arbiters of dietary taste because of its emphasis on local and genuine products, cooked in a fundamentally unfussy and uncomplicated way. For Italians of all classes are connoisseurs of their ingredients: 'Ah', a Tuscan will say, 'that is a good *pecorino* cheese, it is a *pecorino delle pecore della montagna* (a sheep

Fruit and veg displayed with verve

cheese from the sheep on the mountain)'. There *are* still sheep and cattle on the mountains close by and the beef from the Val di Chiana near Arezzo is the foundation of the 'steak Florentine'. Altogether the produce of the Tuscan countryside has an amazing variety. Tuscan dishes are as earthy as the earthenware bowls they are typically served in – sustaining, succulent and rich, unrefined in both senses.

Buying Food

In Florence anyone with the slightest interest in food will want to visit the covered food market (**Mercato Centrale**), close by the **San Lorenzo market** (see p. 97), up the Via dell'Ariento. It is sometimes a deafening place, proffering all kinds of fresh and preserved food from individual stalls on traditional lines. There is

FOOD AND DRINK

Florentine café society

another food market in the streets north of Santa Croce at Piazza Ghiberti (Mercato di Sant'Ambrogio). The only large supermarkets are in the suburbs and though there are a few smaller ones in the centre, food is mainly bought from an *alimentare* or grocer, or a *pizzicheria* or delicatessen.
In towns or villages outside Florence, the once or twice weekly street market in the central square or streets still flourishes – and you cannot do better either for price or for quality. If you are cooking for yourself, even if you undertake nothing more ambitious than pasta, it will taste amazingly different bought fresh and cooked in Italian water (yes, the Italians think that important, too!) with a touch of local olive oil.
In Tuscany, olive oil has the same significance, if not more, as butter or margarine in the

English daily diet (and Italy produces one third of the world's total production). Olive oil is, for instance, commonly eaten with bread, and is also used to transform anything, not just as a cooking oil and to garnish salads. In Tuscany the olive oil of Lucca is regarded as outstanding, although, as usual, each will prefer their local produce. Olive trees are cultivated everywhere in the region and are an essential colour in its wonderful countryside.

Wine
Italy produces more wine than any other country in the world. Until recently the general quality was low, but that has all changed in the last decade. Tuscany itself is home to some famous wines and has several regions

operating DOC (*denominazione di origine controllata*), the Italian's less stringent attempt to copy the French *appellation contrôlée*. A tighter version of DOC, classifying the top quality wines, is the newly created DOCG where G stands for *e Garantita*. By 1985 only five wines had been granted this status and three of these hail from Tuscany.

Best known of Tuscan wines is Chianti which is steadily improving in quality since the introduction of DOCG regulations. There are two styles. The first is a sharp young red, once sold in straw-cradled bottles, though these are rarely seen now – except at demijohn size. The second is the older wine of the top estates. The years 1982, 1983 and 1985 produced particularly good vintages with abundant fruity tastes.

Chianti covers a wide region situated between Florence and Siena (most of it a bit nearer Siena); its more or less official capital is Greve. There are seven sub-regions with Classico and Rufina the most likely to be quoted on wine labels. A Chianti cooperative has offices in Florence and can give detailed information for visits and purchases: Via dei Serragli 146 (tel: (055) 2299351). Or also enquire at the **Enoteca Italiana** in the Fortezza Medicea in Siena (tel: (0577) 288487).

A famous neighbour of Chianti is the similar, though magnified and usually more expensive, Vino Nobile di Montepulciano. Stronger, darker and even more notorious for its high prices is the third DOCG wine – Brunello di Montalcino. A regulatory four years ageing in wooden casks ensures a wine charged with a powerful combination of flavours, tannin and acidity. There are two other wines of note: Carmignano, a wine flavoured with 10 to 15 per cent of Cabernet Sauvignon grapes, is produced to the west of Florence, while Vernaccio di San Gimignano is perhaps Tuscany's best traditional white wine. Now that the habit of mixing large quantities of white juice into Chianti red has disappeared, most producers are using the Trebbiano and Malvasia grapes to produce sharp lemony whites. Galestro is a well-known one but do not expect great value for money.

Take a sip of the grape from a wine seller in a wine cellar

FOOD AND DRINK

However, DOC is far from everything. Always drink the *vino locale* wherever you are in Tuscany: it is part of the scene. It is twice as delicious if you are within spitting distance of the vineyard, and there is a reason why so many Tuscans from field-labourers to business people and doctors make their own or have it made from the vines on their own patch. Most people will be very glad to tell you all about it!

Eating Out

Long ago Tuscany invented the perfect 'nibble', *crostini*, which are served as an *antipasto* or an 'eat-hunger' (*mangiafame*): you might be given some in a restaurant while you are waiting to order. A *crostino* is essentially a piece of toast with something on it, just one thing – a sun-dried tomato in oil, a chicken liver, an olive paste. Otherwise the *antipasto* is commonly a plate of *affettato*, 'sliced' cold meats, from the ubiquitous *prosciutto crudo* (smoked ham, known as Parma ham in English) to the Tuscan speciality of wild boar (*cinghiale*).

The *primi*, the first course, includes pasta (it is worth knowing that 'pasto' in Italian means simply 'meal'; the word for pasta in the English sense is *past'asciutta*, literally 'dried food'). There are as many shapes and kinds of pasta as there are towns in Italy, and then as many sauces as there are villages. You may again be offered wild boar as a sauce, or a *ragù* (which is what we call Bolognese sauce), or a vegetable or seafood flavouring.

In the autumn, if you cannot afford to eat the most expensive mushrooms on their own, you can at least take the crumbs rom the rich man's truffle on your *tagliatelle* (often, here, fleshy and thick ribbon pasta, an excellent vehicle for Tuscan sauces). Other equally nourishing first course dishes are soups and broths, which will be heavy and well loaded with their fresh ingredients. Among these the Tuscan *ribollita* or boil-up of vegetables, featuring especially cabbage, is a famous 'peasant' dish.

Given the emphasis on local fare, the best restaurants offering fish and seafood are usually on the coast, while inland, people eat meat. Florence is famous for its main dish of *bistecca alla fiorentina*, which is usually a T-

bone steak (or rather veal as it is taken from a younger animal than an American steak) grilled with herbs over charcoal. Otherwise, as shooting is a sport about which many Italians are passionate, game should be good, whether wild boar or the humble hare or rabbit. Vegetables are served separately for most dishes, and, as in the rest of Italy, usually lukewarm: they are best thought of as a cooked salad.

After Tuscan *antipasto*, *primo* and main course or *pietanza*, washed down, of course, with local wine, most people will probably have had enough, but sweet dishes are always available, and cheese, and, too, local liqueurs or *digestivi*. In the old days restaurants used often to refuse to serve you unless you had a main course (even at lunchtime), but nowadays it is usually acceptable for customers to eat only pasta (or you may be offered an *assaggio*, a set of different little pasta dishes).

Cakes and Ice-cream
One more Tuscan speciality must be mentioned, though it does not form part of a meal: rather it is taken with coffee between meals. *Panforte*, 'strong bread', is so called because it is a dense concentrate of nuts and honey and some other flavours, sweet, crunchy and filling. A speciality of Siena, it can be bought in many bars or patisseries (*pasticcerie*) throughout Tuscany. Besides this

Palazzo Michelangelo is a perfect watering hole to drink in the sights

FOOD AND DRINK

Food and drink al fresco

and other cakes there will be on sale various *tramezzini* or *panini* (rolls) or *schiacciati* (flat rolls) which in many places can be exquisite.

Last but not least, the ice-cream! Certainly Americans, who understand these things better perhaps than the English, will make an obligatory pilgrimage to the back streets behind the Bargello in Florence to **Vivoli**, Via Isola delle Stinche 7. Old man Vivoli, who was almost a legend in his time, is now dead, and the quality of the extraordinary variety of flavours available can perhaps be equalled elsewhere by this time, but not in many places, even in this land where people commonly eat good ice-cream every day.

Restaurants in Florence

To start at the top, Florence possesses in the **Enoteca Pinchiorri**, Via Ghibellina 87 (tel: 242777) one of the most famous restaurants (and wine cellars) of Europe – at the cost of some people's whole holiday. **Da Noi**, Via Fiésolana 46 (tel: 242917) is in the same school; however, if you are in Florence for a week you should have booked before you came.

Still, Florentines are nothing if not competitive, and there are other restaurants in the city offering excellent fare at less outstanding prices. Generally speaking, the smarter restaurants are found on the outer boulevards of the city, while the cheerful paper-tablecloth variety abound in the centre (both sides of the River Arno), though there are outlying ones as well.

Other restaurants in the plush and pleasant category that will bend but not break a credit card include **Otello**, a long-standing favourite, Via degli Orti Oricellari, on the corner of Via Alamanni (tel: 215819); also by the station **Le Fonticine**, Via Nazionale 79; (tel: 282106); out by San Marco, **Bronzino**, Via delle Ruote 27 (tel: 495220); out in Santa Croce district, **Cibreo**, Via de' Macci 118 (tel: 2341100), for more adventurous gastronomes, which actually offers two sets of prices, in the front of the restaurant or to the back, depending on which side of the kitchen you sit; if you have had enough pasta come here, for it does not serve any. A specialist fish restaurant is **La Capannina di Sante** (upstream by the Arno), Piazza Ravenna

tel: 688345); another, though it
also serves meat, **Pierot**
(downstream across the Arno),
Piazza Taddeo Gaddi 25 (tel:
702100). Another *enoteca* or
vineshop-restaurant besides
Pinchiorri is **Dino**, Via Ghibellina
51 (tel: 241452).

Inside the city centre, for robust,
authentic Tuscan cooking and
genial and sometimes rough
shoulder-rubbing, there is
nowhere better than **Latini**, in the
backstreets behind the Palazzo
Rucellai, Via Palchetti 6 (tel:
210916). Though it is always full
the place extends through
several rooms and has a rapid
turnover. Do not expect a quiet
tête à tête, since tables are
shared. With similar fare and
similarly cheek by jowl is **Coco
Lezzone**, the other side of the Via
Vigna Nova, Via del Parioncino
26 (tel: 287178). Right by the
Ponte Vecchio, there is one of
several cellar restaurants, **Buca
dell'Orafo**, Volta de' Girolami
(tel: 213619); another is **Buca
Lapi**, Via del Trebbio 1 (tel:
213768), known for its *bistecca
fiorentina*. But there are plenty of
less smart but usually very full,
rapid turnover restaurants to be
found all over the centre.
Oltrarno is not quiet 'left bank' in
Florence but it is good for
restaurants and features a couple
resembling bistros, for instance
Mamma Gina, Borgo San Jacopo
37 (tel: 2396009). In the same
street there is also **Cammillo**,
Borgo San Jacopo 57 (tel:
212427) but more friendly and
with better food is the newer
Cinghiale Bianco, Borgo San
Jacopo 43r (tel: 215706). A long
established classic *trattoria* is
Celestino, Piazza Santa Felicità

(tel: 2396574). Though it has
always been there, the *trattoria*
Borgo Antico has nowadays
become very popular with
Florentines, and you can have
just a pizza at Piazza Santo
Spirito (tel: 210437). Of course,
as in the rest of Italy, you can
obtain a snack or sandwich
(*panino*) in any bar, and in many
of them you can get something
very tasty. Then again there are
self-service places or *tavola
calda* offering something more
substantial, and not only those
that line the Via de' Panzani
between the Cathedral and the
station. If they are full, they must
be good; unless you are with a
large party, you will not have to
wait long, although it is advisable
in the evening to reserve or to
set out early. Outside Florence,
one of the delights of Tuscany is
that you will find numerous
wayside restaurants where you
can have a meal *al fresco*
beneath the vine trellises. See
also restaurants in **Siena**,
page 76.

Bars
It has been well said that bars
are the mainstay of Italian life –
not that the Italians are
drunkards, but they purvey
many other things besides
drinks: a telephone for instance,
ice-cream, a sandwich, a cake,
information. They are
everywhere, of all classes. Two
smart bars that make good
meeting-places are **Mokarico** at
Via Calzaiuoli 72 or **Giacosa** on
the corner of Via dei Tornabuoni
and Via della Spada. For ice-
cream **Vivoli**, Via Isola delle
Stinche 7 (behind the Bargello)
is justly famous.

SHOPPING

The art of shop window display is perhaps a secondary aspect of the Italian national genius for design, but it considerably enhances the pleasure of both shopping, and just walking through the streets. In Florence, to ignore the clothes, shoes, antiques and other objects of art and design in the smart shops would be difficult, not to say inhuman. Italians as a nation spend more per capita on clothes (and such things) than the rest of us and their reward is an enormous variety and choice of beautiful things to buy. Virtually any shops you need in Florence, apart from ironmongers and car-dealers, can be found in the centre of the city, either side of the **Ponte Vecchio** – which is itself a sequence of shops specialising in jewellery (see p. 43). It is the only street to retain in this way its historic specialisation, although the Gucci shops are not very far from the **Via dei Calzaiuoli**, Street of the Cobblers. Florence is the place to shop: other Tuscan cities cannot offer anything like the same quantity or variety.

Unfortunately, these beautiful things are not cheap, and they are no longer even comparatively less expensive – or, even though Italy's political troubles have weakened the value of the *lira* in recent times, inflation has continued unceasingly on its way. In certain areas, above all leather goods like handbags and shoes, it used

The Duomo exemplifies the Florentines' flair for design

to be cheaper to buy in Italy but anyone looking for that kind of bargain today is liable to be disillusioned. The only compensation is that the quality – as well as the chic – remains and the goods are still good value. That said, be careful to count the noughts: it does happen that something looks quite reasonable at L100,000 but actually is L1,000,000 – £500 not £50!

Antiques
Though they are hardly suitable items for taking home in your suitcase, Florence is particularly famed for its furniture, craft shops and workshops. In the backstreets many cabinet-makers are to be seen at work, on traditional designs, reproduction pieces and restoration. It is not always easy to define which. Museums the world over have in their basements a few more items than they wanted of Florentine art – fakes, in other words, in which the Florentines are meant to be past masters, if that is the right phrase.
Look for shops down the **Via dei Fossi** between Santa Maria Novella and the river, then along the **Lungarno** towards the Ponte Vecchio; across the Ponte Santa Trinità along **Via Maggio** or down **Borgo Sant'Jacopo** back to the Ponte Vecchio.

Books, Reproductions and Stationery
Florence is a beautiful city, not only in reality but also on the printed page. It is the home of two of the most famous photographic houses in the world, **Alinari**, with its enormous black-and-white archive of art

SHOPPING

and architecture, and the more recent **Scala**, known for its high-quality colour repro. Alinari is now installed in the Palazzo Rucellai (see p. 40) in Via della Vigna Nuova; Scala has a shop ('**al Cupolone**'), Piazza del Duomo 60. But the city abounds with bookshops and bookstalls – and in Florence you can buy art books from newspaper stalls. A handsome book or some fine marbled paper or other 'art' stationery, as sold in speciality shops, might be an appropriate souvenir of the city. Look around the same central streets as for clothes, but also on the other side of the Ponte Vecchio as well.

Clothes, Shoes and Leather Goods

Milan is the *couturier* capital, but fashion goes on everywhere in Italy and not least in Florence. Despite the dominance these days of national and Euro-designers, the shops in Florence have a distinctive elegance and there is the added advantage that the clothes are being modelled all around you, if you are looking for ideas. Any designer will be glad to add Florence to his 'London–Paris–Milan–New York–Tokyo' label, and anybody who is anybody and several who are only Italian (for instance **Luisa**, who has a couple of shops in Florence) have outlets here. The **Gucci** were a Florentine family, and there is still a high proportion of leather-goods shops.

Smart shops abound down and off the central **Via dei Calzaiuoli** and **Via dei Tornabuoni**, down to the Ponte Vecchio and along beside the river. For cheaper

goods try the **San Lorenzo market** (see below) and for cheaper shoes in particular the streets between San Lorenzo and the **Via dei Panzani**.

Food and General

Apart from street markets or the central market (see p. 87) you must buy food from *alimentari* or grocers (often also called *pizzicheria*), which will mostly have the usual supermarket items as well – tissues, tampons, toothpaste and shoe polish. General purpose shops or ironmongers are known in Tuscany as *mesticheria*.

In Italy as in France tobacco is a licensed government concession and is sold in *tabacchi* shops, marked outside by a white T

Shopping may call for belt-tightening

against a blue background.
These also sell stamps and
stationery.

Markets and Department
Stores

If your idea of shopping is
finding a bargain, then Florence
once again tries to oblige with its
lively and friendly markets.
Prices are indeed reasonable
but nothing is exactly given
away. There is a smaller one in
the **Mercato Nuovo** on the road
leading to the Ponte Vecchio, but
the largest is behind **San
Lorenzo**. Round the open side of
the church, clogging your way to
the entrance to Michelangelo's
Medici Chapel, are numerous
stalls selling bags, belts and lace
and so on. For the addict, on

Tuesday morning there is a
market in the **Cascine Park** past
the Ponte della Vittoria.
The household-name Italian
chain department store is
Standa; comparison is
dangerous, but if you buy socks
in Marks and Spencers in Britain
then buy them in Italy in Standa.
Its rival **Upim** is a little cheaper,
but it tends to show. **Coin** is
more expensive but also has
more interesting and classier
clothes.
Standa: one branch is at Via
Panzani 31, the road between the
Cathedral and the station, but
there are others further out;
Upim: Via degli Speziali 3–23;
Coin: Via de' Calzaiuoli 56.

ACCOMMODATION

Arriving without accommodation
To help you there is a hotel cooperative at **Florence station** which will find you a hotel (*open*: 08.30 to 20.00hrs most of the year: only in the morning in low season), or at the **Fortezza da Basso** parking-lot during the summer; also one in **Siena** by **San Domenico**, opposite the coach-stop. (You must go in person to these places; they will not make bookings for you over the telephone.) Tourist offices will also assist.

Italian hotels are strictly registered and controlled, so fundamentally you get what you pay for and there should be no unpleasant surprises. There is an official star system going up to five (and then a special de luxe category) but one-star hotels are rare. Two-star hotels or *pensioni* are perfectly adequate. *Pensioni* are really boarding-houses and have been a feature of Florence for many years. The most traditional are characterised by their old-fashioned, domestic atmosphere, sporting gleaming parquet floors and highly polished antique furniture, but not all are like this. *Pensioni* cater for the majority of people coming to Florence as three-star hotels are quite costly.

It is best to book in advance if you know your plans, but in Florence or Tuscany it is not difficult to find somewhere to stay except in high season (Easter, July and August) or except during a special event: get organised beforehand if you want to stay in Siena during its major festival. Most hotels do group rates, and many will do a special family price. In low season you might try bargaining.

Villa Holidays

It is now easy to find a villa holiday in Tuscany at almost any travel agent, and the Italian Tourist Office in your own country's capital will send you a list of agents if you have special requirements. Villas range from the very grand with frescoed interiors and run-down palatial exteriors to converted cowsheds or ultra-modern with swimming pools. There has been a tradition of letting villas to tourists ever since the Grand Tour became an important part of a cultured person's education in the 18th century. The range of villas has greatly increased in recent years as tourism has expanded. What is called *agriturismo* (staying on the farm; there are varieties where you work on the farm, too!) is booming in Italy, so that letting services are increasing and improving all the time. A flight from the land in the years after World War II had left many farmhouses empty, while rigid rent and eviction laws encouraged house-owners to look for foreign and short lets; now the squeeze on European agriculture had made occupant farmers, too, look for extra income in lettings. That is not to count the English who own houses in Tuscany or 'Chiantishire' as it has been called. It should be possible to find something idyllic, for the Tuscan countryside, it bears repeating, is extremely beautiful;

also you will be able to drink the wine from the farm vineyard and eat the local produce. However, you will certainly need a car to get about.

Hotels in Florence

In Florence, many hotels occupy two or three floors of mansion blocks that are also used for offices or apartments. It is therefore difficult to form an impression without going in, but do not worry about the anonymous exterior. Some modest *pensioni* can in fact be quite palatial (star-ratings depend largely on the number and nature of the bathrooms, etc, not on aesthetic quality). As anywhere in Italy, noise is extremely difficult to avoid, and even if there is no traffic you may well be woken in the still dawn by the sound of refuse collection!

Expensive Hotels

Two grand hotels in Florence face each other: **Excelsior**, Piazza Ognissanti 3 (tel: 264201) and the refurbished **Grand**, Piazza Ognissanti 1 (tel: 288781). Both have piano cocktail bars. The super de luxe hotel in Florence is up in Fiésole, the **Villa San Michele**, Via Doccia 4, Fiésole (tel: 59451). A slightly less exorbitant 'park' hotel offering family accommodation and gardens is the **Villa Cora**, Via le Machiavelli 18 (tel: 2298451). Business hotels include the **Annalena**, Via Romana 34 (tel: 222402) and the **Palazzo Pitti**, Via Barbadori 2 (tel: 2398711).

Reasonable Hotels

The following listed hotels are essentially *pensioni* (two or three-star) rather than de luxe hotels, but score heavily for old-world venerability, architecture and traditional decor, etc.
Loggiato dei Serviti, a former convent opposite Brunelleschi's Ospedale (see p. 38), Piazza Santissima Annunziata 3 (tel: 289592).
Hermitage, Vicolo Marzio 1, Piazza del Pesce (tel: 287216).
Jennings-Riccioli, the original hotel of E M Forster's book and the film set in Florence of *Room with a View*, Corso Tintori 7 (tel: 244751).
Quivisana e Ponte Vecchio, where they actually made the film *Room with a View*, Lungarno Archibusieri 4 (tel: 216692/215046).
Beacci Tornabuoni, Via Tornabuoni 3, (tel: 212645).

Hotels come with a view in Florence

Two other tasteful places but a little less expensive are **Aprile**, Via della Scala 6 (tel: 216237/289147) and **Alba**, Via della Scala 22 (tel: 282610).

Inexpensive Hotels

In the basic two-star category there is an enormous choice but little to choose between it all. The essential criterion is probably location, though most are fairly central.

Sometimes in major cities the hotels round the station are unsavoury, but this is not really the case in Florence.

In the two-star category you can usually opt for a room with or without an adjoining bathroom with shower. You will be lucky to find a bath anywhere below three stars, and if you want one you must ask specifically. All these *pensioni* take groups, and around Easter (the great time for school trips) they will be full of school-children.

One to be recommended for decent value and service is the **Patrizia**, Via Montebello 7 (tel: 282314).

Youth Hostels

There are two youth hostels in Florence, the **Villa Camerata**, Viale Righi 2–4 (tel: 601451), where you will be required to show your youth hostel card, and the **Santa Monica**, Via Santa Monica 6 (tel: 268338), where you may be let in anyway. Both should be booked well in advance in high season, by telephone. Also the **Villa Favard**, Via Rocca Tedalda, is available June to September; there are no beds but it's useful for sleeping-bag users.

CULTURE, ENTERTAINMENT, NIGHTLIFE

Florence is not a resort, nor is it a trendy metropolis: people do not usually come for the discos and if they have they will be disappointed. If that is true of the capital of the region, it is even truer elsewhere. Florence does however offer some 'nightlife' in the form of the rather formal and rather expensive, nightclub/disco establishment: **Space Electronic**, Via Palazzuolo, (tel: 293082) and **Yab Yum**, Via Sassetti 5 (tel: 282018).

A much more popular form of entertainment, as in all Italian cities, is the promenade, when it seems the whole world takes to the street for an evening stroll and to watch the rest of the world go by from a pavement café. Favourite places in Florence are the Piazza della Repubblica and the Ponte Vecchio. This is the haunt of the young, who play guitars and make or watch street entertainment, such as acrobatics, clowning or magic shows.

There are some museums that are opened in the evenings between 21.00 and 23.00 hours on a few evenings a month, including the **Cathedral Museum**, the **Casa Buonarroti** and the **Palazzo Vecchio**. A brochure is available from the Tourist Offices to give details of any additional venues.

If your Italian is up to it, there are plays at the **Teatro dell'Oriuolo**, Via dell'Oriuolo (tel: 2340507) and a revue theatre, **Teatro Verdi** on Via Ghibellina (tel:

CULTURE, ENTERTAINMENT, NIGHTLIFE

Talking: the great Italian pastime

2396242). During November there is a special theatre season. Tuscany as a whole is quite musical, and Florence is no exception. The *Maggio Musicale Fiorentino* festival during May and June includes international performers and the *Firenze Estate* during the remainder of the summer offers a variety of musical and other cultural events.

Concerts are often held in a church or fine palace, so that the harmonious surroundings may enhance the performance. Music is performed in fact in various different 'seasons' or one-off performances in a variety of different places. The **Teatro della Pergola**, Via della Pergola 12/32 (tel: 2479651) will give information and sell tickets for other musical and cultural events in the city as well as its own.

Outside Florence, at **Fiésole** there is a better-known *Estate* with performances in the Roman amphitheatre. In **Siena**, which has a musical academy, there are plenty of musical events. Information can be obtained from the **Accademia Musicale Chigiana**, Via della Citta 82 (tel: (0577) 46152) or at the Tourist Office. There is also an opera festival at **Barga** during July and August.

There are many cinemas in Florence, showing usually the same range of films as in the rest of Europe but some a little earlier, others a little later, than they are released elsewhere. They are usually dubbed, but the cinema **Astro**, Piazza San Simone (tel: 222588) shows English-language films undubbed.

WEATHER AND WHEN TO GO

Mediterranean Italy enjoys a generally mild climate and warm summers. That said, there can be great exceptions. The most common false assumption people make is that Italy is warmer in spring and winter than is northern Europe. The truth is, that the autumn lasts longer and although October can be very pleasant, and it is often possible to eat outside in the sun on 1 December, once winter has set in it usually gets very cold, colder even than in the north. Italy is also slow to warm up again, so that people arriving in Tuscany for Easter expecting to find the summer having begun can be severely disappointed, and can freeze in the biting winds. On the other hand there is usually plenty of sun all year round, spring, summer, autumn and winter, so even though you have to wear an overcoat, it all looks very beautiful.

Summer can be very warm, but Tuscany is far enough north and mountainous enough to keep reasonably cool – it usually avoids the sweltering heat of Rome and southern Italy, and the very high humidity. Central Italy, however, has pockets of different climates and so, while Florence, which sits in a basin, can be insufferably hot, the surrounding hills can still be pleasantly cool.

In August Florence can be decidedly unpleasant as the surrounding hills make it very hot indeed. Any Italian free to do so will have taken to the hills or gone to the coast.

When Easter is fine – but you cannot rely on it – it can be radiantly fine, and is one of the best times to visit Italy. If you want to avoid crowds and your prime purpose is to visit the art and architecture, you will be better advised to go out of season. January and February are the quietest months. Be warned that October is not out of season and the end of October in particular can be very busy. Easter is a pleasant time to visit, but be prepared not only for the cold but for school-children in large and noisy numbers.

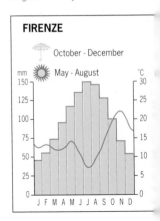

FIRENZE

October - December

mm May - August ˚C

HOW TO BE A LOCAL

What you look like is what you are – this is as true in Italy as the proverb 'manners maketh man'. Looking good, dressing well, presenting yourself well pay real dividends: in a word they earn respect. Looking smart and decent can make the difference, for instance, between a good table and bad one, quick service and being ignored, gaining entry from an attendant or not, and so on. Italians in general, but Florentines in particular, simply disdain the ugly or untidy – and they almost unconsciously discriminate against them. A possible comparison might be to table manners: some people are easily upset by poor table manners, but Italians not – indeed their table manners are often appalling by other nations' standards. So don't worry about how you spoon your spaghetti, but do up your shirt!

Slovenly Anglo-Saxons will be amazed when they arrive for the first time in Florence and see how well everyone is dressed – everyone, rich or poor, on the buses or in a taxi, from shop assistants to business people. There is an enormous contrast to the streets, say, of Britain, because visual awareness is every bit as much an Anglo-Saxon defect as it is an Italian talent. Non-Italians seem often to dress so as not to be seen, but Italians always look. Most people, therefore, will have some catching-up to do. If the Italians have a fault when it comes to clothes, it is that they are slaves to fashion, so do not be afraid to imitate what you see around you.

If you doubt your taste, you can seek advice. This is true in fact of everything. Though Tuscans are known to some extent for their rough and ready ways, no Italian resents being asked a question, indeed Italians like to be asked things, and are always asking themselves. Some people, for example, will normally read the signs or signposts to get information; Italians will invariably ask someone, even if there are notices all over the place. Italians will usually talk in trains, while other nationalities seldom do. It is also true that Italians are always pleased when foreigners take an interest in them and their culture. They will also respond kindly when you try to speak their language. So ask anyway. That said, stupid questions will earn you the same kind of distancing as being badly dressed will.

Personal appearance is one of the things that come up early in Italian conversations – in whatever language they may be conducted. Italians will quickly compliment you on some personal aspect, and you may do the same! Italians will very readily tell someone they are good-looking – or not! – in a way that may seem forward to others. They lose their tempers quickly – and then get over it just as rapidly – and are candid and frank. They say what they think, and will expect you to do the same. Do so clearly and forcefully – Italians can't hear mumblers, and theirs is a highly enunciated language. Both adults and children are freer to make much more noise in Italy.

CHILDREN, SPORT AND LEISURE

City holidays with children can be difficult as their tolerance of museums, galleries and historic buildings is limited. Florence does offer sights for them such as the Forte di Belvedere with its massive ramparts and views over Florence; this is next to the Boboli Gardens which is a lovely park with fountains, a grotto and an amphitheatre. There are several museums which can be of interest to children such as the Museum of the History of Science in the Palazzo dei Guidici, the Museo Storico Topografico with its exhibition of 'How Florence used to be' or the Zoological Museum in the Palazzo Torrigiani.

The opportunity for swimming is always welcomed and Florence has several open-air swimming pools:

Piscina Comunale Bellariva, Lungarno Colombo 6
Piscina Costoli, Viale Paoli
Piscina Poggetto, Via Michele Marcati 24b
Piscina Le Pavionere, Via delle Cascine.

Outside the city there is easy access to miles of beach on the Tuscan coast. Resort centres are Viareggio to the north and Orbetello to the south; there is also the island of Elba for a longer expedition. Among many other places, Castiglioncello south of Livorno is a particularly pleasant spot among the pine trees, though it has rocks instead of sand.

There is plenty of countryside surrounding the city for walks and picnics. Italians are great countryside walkers and there is plenty of information on the region from **Club Alpino Italiano**, Via dello Studio 5, Florence (tel: 211731).

Sport

When it comes to sport, football, as the World Cup of 1990 made very clear, is the Italian national sport. Every city has a stadium, including Florence. Basketball is also popular, and both get wide coverage on television.

The Piscina Costoli mentioned above is part of Florence's enormous sports complex, **Campo di Marte**, which also has a 55,000 seat stadium, tennis courts, baseball pitch, basketball and other sporting facilities.

Florence has two racecourses by the Cascine Park, and a golf club, **Golf dell'Ugolino** about seven and a half miles (12km) outside the city (Grassina, Strada Chiantigiana 3).

For sporting facilities/events, enquire at your hotel or at the Tourist Office (and get them to arrange it). In winter, Tuscany can offer skiing, at the resorts of Abetone and Cutigliano in the Apennines to the north.

A little relaxation after some exhausting shopping

IGHT BUDGET

is sad but true that Italy is no
nger relatively cheap; in many
ays it is more expensive now
an France. Accommodation,
od, and admission charges in
articular have risen in the last
ecade well beyond the official
te of inflation. The only
fective way of saving money is
go without. However, here are
few more or less obvious
oservations:

Stay outside the centre, or not
Florence at all. Hotels and
ensioni are cheaper in the
naller cities of Tuscany. Youth
ostels and camping sites are
heaper still.

In Florence, eat in the
rowded, rapid-turnover
staurants. You may have to
ait, and you may be squashed
, but the bill will be lighter and
e food good value.

Restaurants nowadays rarely

*A little of what you fancy could mean
digging deep into your pocket; it
costs less to stand and stare*

insist that you have a main
course as well as pasta. Meat is
particularly expensive, and the
main course is seldom
garnished. Do without! Or have a
plate of local cheese instead.
● Avoid bars in prominent
positions and with chairs and
tables outside. Look instead in
the back-streets. If your back is
aching, there are quite a number
of small bars with a few seats
inside but which do not charge
extra for sitting in them.
Otherwise, where the seats and
tables have a view, there is a
considerable mark-up and
waiter service is compulsory. If a
waiter is involved, the standard
mark-up is 100 per cent. If you
do use a waiter, no need to leave
a tip – you have already paid for
his services!

● If you are trying to save money on food, eat ice-cream! Apart from being filling, it is very good and usually reasonable in Italy, so long as it comes from a scoop and not a packet.

● Buy a picnic rather than a sit-down lunch or a snack in a bar. The problem in Florence is that there are few places to eat it in peace.

SPECIAL EVENTS

Tuscany is rich in festivals and processions, which have been in many cases deliberately fostered since the 19th century. The most famous and colourful of them all is the **Palio** of Siena (see **Siena**). This spectacular three-lap bareback horse race around the Campo is the liveliest fiesta in Italy. It is held twice a year in July and August, though the August event is meant to be the more important one. The comparable event in **Florence** is the historic football match played on 24 June, the **Feast-day of St John the Baptist**, Florence's patron saint. The game is played in historic dress, after a lot of parading. The players have to score goals, but there are no rules about how. Other examples are the **Balestra del Girifalco**, or Falcon's Joust, held in costume in the town of **Massa Maritima** on the Sunday on or after 20 May and on the second Sunday in August; and the **Giostra del Saracino** held on the first Sunday in September in **Arezzo**. All these will usually be accompanied by evening fireworks. To cheer the winter up, in February **Carnevale** is celebrated more or less riotously everywhere particularly at

Viaréggio – but nowhere as in Venice where it was originally revived about a decade ago having been suppressed by the French in 1797.

Religious Festivals

Other feasts in the area are more strictly religious: perhaps the best-known is the procession – accompanied by an influx from the countryside, street stalls, and general rejoicing – of the **Volto Santo** (an 11th-century wooden image of Christ) in **Lucca** on 13 September. In **Florence**, Easter Sunday is celebrated with the **Scoppio del Carro**, in which the main focus is the dove, or *columba*, which zooms on a wire across the packed Cathedral in a very jovial atmosphere. Most such secular or religious feasts occur in summer, in July, August or September. **Assumption Day** (15 August) has always been celebrated as a day of fair and festival all over Italy.

Wine Festivals

In September many wine festivals are held more or less spontaneously in the countryside, not only with wine to be drunk and for sale, but with all sorts of stalls selling food.

Music Festivals

Classical music festivals include a festival of sacred music held in Lucca during May, Florence's **Maggio Musicale** or Musical May, with many invited performers, Siena's July music festival at the **Accademia Musicale Chigiana**, and the opera festival held in August in the pretty village of Barga.

DIRECTORY

Contents

Arriving at Santa Maria Novella

Arriving

Italy is an EC country and has no special entry regulations; it no longer has currency regulations. The main airport for Florence and Tuscany is at Pisa (**Galileo Galilei Airport**), though there are charter flights landing at Peretola, a couple of miles outside Florence. Air UK has a flight from Stansted direct to Florence.

Pisa airport is over 50 miles (80km) away from Florence, so taking a taxi can be expensive! There is a direct rail link between Florence and Pisa airport at least every hour. Allow an hour for the train journey. Airport information: tel: (050) 500707 or (055) 216073. Though Pisa is not a large airport it has banks, a restaurant, and a small duty-free shop.

Florence's main station is **Santa Maria Novella**, close to the centre of the city. It is a terminus with daily (at least) 'intercity' and sleeper connections to other cities in Italy and Europe. Driving and parking in the city centre is severely restricted. The main reception car park is at the **Fortezza da Basso** (signposted on the route in from the motorway); there is also a large underground car park located at the main railway station.

Camping

The Italians are keen campers, so there are many camping sites with well-kept facilities. Information is easily obtained at local tourist offices or before you go at the Italian Tourist Office. The main campsites for Florence are **Italiani e Stranieri**, Viale Michelangelo 80 (tel: 6811977; *open*: April–September) or **Villa Camerata** (also the youth hostel) Via Righi 2–4, tel: 601451: if you do not book, arrive early.

Car Rental

In Florence the main agencies are all close together, three in Borgo Ognissanti: Avis, Borgo Ognissanti 128r (tel: 213629/2398826); Europcar, Borgo Ognissanti 53r (tel: 2360072/294130); Italy by Car, Borgo Ognissanti 134r (tel: 293021/287161), and two more round the corner in Via Finiguerra: Hertz, Via Finiguerra 33r (tel: 2398205/282260) and Maggiore, Via Finiguerra 11r (tel: 210238/294578). There are also offices at Pisa airport: Autotravel (tel: 050 46209); Avis

(tel: 050 42028); Europcar (tel: 050 41017); Maggiore (tel: 050 42574). Maggiore also have an office at Peretola airport (Florence). For other towns look under 'Autonoleggio' in the *Pagine Gialle* (Yellow Pages).

Chemist see Pharmacies

Crime

Any tourist centre is liable to crimes like pickpocketing, but the situation is better in Florence than in larger centres such as Milan, Rome or Naples. In particular there is little of that favourite Italian street crime, the *scippo* or snatch, often from a passing motorcycle. To avoid being an obvious target, see **Personal Safety**. Take great care to lock your car and avoid leaving anything valuable visible. Italians often remove their car radios and carry them with them. If you are insured, you are required to inform the police within 24 hours in order to make a claim when you return. Do so at a police station or *questura* and obtain a statement or *denuncia* (see **Police**).

Customs Regulations

Allowances have largely been abolished since January 1992 for nationals of EC countries. Other visitors are entitled to the following allowances (aged 17 years or over):

Tobacco

300 cigarettes *or* 75 cigars *or* 400 grams of tobacco

Alcohol

1 litre of spirits or strong liqueurs (over 22% volume) *or* 2 litres of fortified or sparkling wine, or low strength liqueurs

Plus
2 litres of still table wine

Perfume
50 grams

Toilet Water
250 cc

Other goods
Items bought in Italy up to the value of 1,000,000 *lire* may be exported duty-free. For goods exceeding this value an application to export must be presented to Customs.
In addition, items for *personal use* may be temporarily imported into Italy free of duty. For goods obtained duty- and tax-paid in the European Community, the above allowances are increased.

Disabled Visitors
Florence is not ideal for unaccompanied wheelchair travel and there are few provisions made for the disabled.
Some major attractions, like the Uffizi, are accessible to wheelchairs, but others are not. A list of hotels in Florence from the Italian State Tourist Board (1 Princes Street, London W1R 8AY) (tel: (071) 408 1254)) marks those convenient for disabled visitors with the wheelchair sign. Radar (12 City Forum, 250 City Road, London EC1V 8AF, tel: (071) 250 3222) offers general advice on travel and accommodation abroad. For a fact sheet on travel for disabled people in Italy, send a large SAE to Holiday Care Service, 2 Old Bank Chambers, Station Road, Horley, Surrey RH6 9HW (tel: (0293) 774535).

Driving

Petrol
Petrol is more expensive in Italy than in England or than in most European countries.
Credit cards are rarely acceptable at petrol stations. All except small garages in out-of-the-way places have unleaded petrol, in pumps marked *senza piombo*.
Do not get caught with an empty tank (in rural areas particularly) between 12.00 and 15.00 hours or after 19.00 hours when many petrol stations are closed. If you carry a 'green' UK driving licence get hold of an official Italian translation (from motoring organizations) to accompany it. EC 'pink' licences are acceptable without translation. A green card (International Motor Insurance Certificate) is strongly recommended for Italy.

Motoring regulations
In Florence, all motor vehicles are banned from the city centre between 07.30 and 18.30 hours, Monday to Saturday. If your hotel is in this area and you arrive by car, you'll be allowed to stop outside for unloading – and must then park elsewhere! Do not park in front of any signs saying '*Divieto di Sosta*' (No Parking), or your vehicle may be towed away. Requisitioned car park (where cars are towed when parked illegally): Via Dell'Arcovata 6 (tel: 355231). Seatbelts are compulsory in front and rear seats (where equipped) and children must use a belt or a child restraint whether in the front or rear. Motorcyclists must wear helmets.

Look out for other road users

In the case of a breakdown, ring 116 (nationwide), which will put you in touch with the nearest ACI (Automobile Club d'Italia) garage. (The ACI head office is at Via Marsala 8, 00 18 5 Rome, tel: (06) 49981, with branches in most large towns.) The ACI emergency breakdown service (towing to the nearest ACI garage) is free to vehicles bearing a foreign registration (or a rented vehicle from either Rome or Milan international airport); you will need to produce your passport (also rental contract and flight ticket if appropriate).

Always, in the event of a breakdown, a red warning triangle must be displayed 55 yards (50 metres) behind the vehicle and flashing hazard lights must be turned on.

Full beam headlights may only be used outside towns and use of the horn in built-up areas is banned, except in cases of immediate danger. (At night, flashing headlights can be used instead.) Outside town, however, the horn is compulsory as a warning of hazard ahead. Maximum speed limits are 31mph (50kph) in built-up areas, 56mph (90kph) on secondary roads and, 68mph (110kph) on main roads and motorways. For cars towing trailers or caravans, the respective figures are 44mph (70kph) and 50mph (80kph). In addition keep your eyes open for local speed limit variations. Fines for traffic offences may be demanded on the spot by traffic police.

Road signs are mostly international though the following may be useful for first-time drivers in Italy:

Rallentare – slow down
Senso Vietato – no entry

Sosta Autorizzata/Vietata –
parking permitted/no parking
Svolta – a bend in the road
Incrocio – cross-roads
benzina senza piombo –
unleaded petrol.

Electricity
The supply is 220 volts AC (50
cycles), though any British,
Australian or New Zealand
appliances normally requiring a
slightly higher voltage, will work.
For visitors from the US or
Canada with appliances
normally requiring 100/120 volts,
and not fitted for dual-voltage, a
voltage transformer is required.
Plugs are of two pins (of two
different types or sizes) or
sometimes three pins set
vertically in a row, so an
international adaptor is needed.

Embassies and Consulates
National embassies to Italy are in
Rome, but most European
countries and some American
ones have consulates in
Florence.
British Consulate, Lungarno
Corsini 2 (tel: (055)
284133/212594).
United States Consulate:
Lungarno Vespucci 38 (tel: (055)
2398276).
No consulates for Eire, Australia
or Canada, but their embassies
in Rome have these nos:
Eire (tel: 06-6782541-5)
Australia (tel: 06-852721)
Canada (tel: 06-8415341).

Emergency Telephone Numbers
For an emergency of any kind,
dial 113.
Specifically for a fire (*Vigili di
Fuoco*) 115.

For a medical emergency
(*pronto soccorso*) 118;
ambulance 212222/215555.
For the police (*Carabinieri*) 112.
For an English-speaking doctor
ask the British or US consulate
(see **Embassies and
Consulates**) or dial 116.

Entertainment Information
In the larger cities the hotel
association usually publishes a
free booklet ('concierge
information') featuring current
and upcoming events: you will
probably find one in your room
if you are staying in a hotel. In
Florence there are *Florence
Today* and *Chiavi d'Oro*.
Otherwise the local Tourist
Office will be full of posters and
information about special events.

Health
Nationals of the EC can take
advantage of Italy's health
service. If you are British, before
you set off, get hold of form E111
from the Post Office, which
covers EC residents for medical
treatment in Italy. (Ask your
travel agent or apply to the Post
Office directly for the leaflet
Medical Costs Abroad, which
contains an application for E111.)
You must present E111, should
the need arise at a Local Health
Unit (*Unità Sanitaria Locale*)
before you seek treatment in
Italy. Full details on procedure
and benefits will be issued with
E111, which does not cover all
medical expenses and will not
pay for your repatriation. You
should, therefore, also take out a
separate holiday insurance
policy to cover such
emergencies.
The high cost of medical

treatment makes travel insurance **essential** if you are a **non-EC citizen**. For medical treatment and medicines, keep all bills to claim the money back later. There are no special health regulations for visitors to Florence. You can, if you wish, check that none are in force at the time you wish to travel by contacting the Health Authorities of the country from which you are travelling or by telephoning the Travel Clinic (tel: (071) 499 4000). It is advisable to be up to date with tetanus injections. Mosquito repellent, however, is a must and some form of sun protection is necessary as the summer sun can be very fierce. It is also advisable to drink bottled water and to wash all fruit and vegetables.

If you should have a minor ailment, chemists (*farmacia*) can give advice and dispense prescriptions (see **Pharmacies**).

Lost Property

The lost property office (Ufficio Oggetti Smarriti) in Florence is at Via Circondaria 19 (tel: (055) 367943). If you lost the item on a train, then enquire at the office (Ufficio Oggetti Rinvenuti) on Santa Maria Novella station (tel: (055) 2352190).

Money Matters

The currency in Italy is the Italian *lira* (plural *lire*). This is abbreviated to LIT. An attempt in the Italian parliament to knock some of the noughts off the *lira* failed recently, so the tourist

Horse and carriage in Piazza della Signoria

Hi-tech bureau de change

must just get used to counting in thousands and millions.

Currently, the lira is likely to stay valued at approximately LIT 2,500 against the pound sterling. As a rule of thumb, take three noughts off and halve it: 1,000 lire is just under 50p and 1,000,000 lire is a little under £500. An American dollar is about 1,700 *lire* so just take three noughts off. Notes come in denominations of 1,000, 2,000, 5,000, 10,000, 50,000 and 100,000. There is usually no trouble changing a 50,000 note (roughly the equivalent of £20), but it is a bit much to try to buy a coffee with a 100,000 note. Coins come in denominations of 50 (now virtually useless), 100, 200 and 500 you used also to be given *gettoni* or telephone tokens, which are perfectly acceptable alternatives to 200 lire (as long as that remains the price of a local call). Currency restrictions entering Italy have now been lifted. The visitor can export up to the equivalent of 20 million lira (amounts in excess of this figure can be exported provided they

have been declared at entry on Form V2).

Italian fascination with high-tech has meant that Florence has led the way in providing automat currency exchange machines which work well with cash. All banks should take Eurocheques as well as travellers' cheques; some of them will give cash on a Visa or other credit card.

Banking hours are 08.30 to 13.20 hours, Monday to Friday (go before 09.00 hours to avoid a queue), and many also open 15.00 to 16.00 hours.

Several travel agents (CIT, Primavera, Wagon Lits, Lazzi Express, Intertravel, Universal) also change money. A bank at the station is open all day 08.20 to 18.20 hours, and at Pisa airport similar hours (depending on flights) and normally your own hotel will be glad to change money.

Credit cards are widely accepted without any problem in most dry goods shops. Expect to pay cash for food except in smart restaurants, and for petrol.

Opening Times

Shops
Generally open from 09.00 to 13.00 hours in the morning, then 16.00 to 20.00 hours (in summer) or 15.00 to 19.00 hours (in winter). Clothes shops and the like are closed on Monday morning.

Banks
These are not open on Saturdays or Sundays. They are open Monday to Friday 08.30 to 13.20 hours. Some also open between 15.00 and 16.00 hours. See **Money Matters**.

Museums
There is no rule, but state museums usually close on Monday and smaller museums tend to open only in the mornings. Museums also close on public holidays. They are also prone to sudden closures as a result of staff shortages, strikes or renovation.

Churches
These usually open early in the morning and close at 12.00 or 12.30 hours; they seldom open in the afternoon before 15.30 and then close about 19.00 hours. Well known tourist churches (see **What to See**) may have longer hours, and out-of-the-way ones may not open at all except on request (best in the morning).

Personal Safety
These days nobody likes to walk alone after dark, but Florence and Tuscany are law-abiding and much safer than many other countries. The streets do not become deserted until about midnight and though

San Francesco della Francesca, Arezzo

streetwalkers and the like come out in the late evening, they hardly pose a threat. There is no reason why women alone should have any particular problem, although Italians like naturally to talk to strangers, it would be foolish to take unnecessary risks. If you are alone and it is late or you are not sticking to the main thoroughfares, it would be wiser to take a taxi. See also **Crime**.

Pharmacies
Pharmacies (*farmacia*) are distinguished by a green cross. They sell medicines rather more exclusively than English chemists (for shampoo, etc., you should go to a general shop or a *profumeria*) and their pharmacist can prescribe more freely. All night chemists are to be found in Florence at the station (Comunale, tel: 289435) and at the hospital of Santa Maria Nuova. Also often open late are the pharmacies at Via Calzaiuoli 7r (Molteni, tel: 289490) and in Piazza San Giovanni 20r (Taverna, tel: 284013). Usually the local chemist will display in its window the nearest chemist which is open out of normal hours.

Places of Worship
If you are Catholic and know Italian, there is no problem. Catholic services in English are held in the Duomo (Florence Cathedral) on Saturday at 17.00 hours. In Florence, the American church (St James) is at Via Rucellai 13 (tel: 294417). The Anglican church (St Mark) is at Via Maggio 16 (tel: 294764). The

Methodist church is at Via de' Benci 9 (tel: 2477800). Jehovah's Witnesses are at Via Val di Chiana 68 (tel: 4221606) and several other places. A synagogue is at Via Farini 4 (tel: 245252).

Police

In an emergency dial 113. There are four sorts of Italian police: the *Vigili Urbani*, the *Carabinieri*, the *Polizia di Stato* (state police) and the *Guardia di Finanza*. The last are rather like the Fraud Squad and the CID – for high-powered crime. The *Carabinieri* (armed) are a force of the Italian army, dealing with theft, road accidents, etc. The *Vigili Urbani* are there to be asked the way, to stop you parking, to help children across the road, and so on.

A *Carabinieri* police station is called a *Caserma*, a *Polizia di Stato* station is called a *Questura*. If you want to report a crime the vital word is *denuncia* ('dehnooncha'). That means something has to be written down. You will be able to do so in English on a multi-lingual form. For the Foreigners and Immigration Section, Via Zara 2 (tel: 49771).

Post Offices

The central Post Office is in Via Pellicceria by Piazza della Repubblica and is open from 08.15 to 18.00 hours, Monday to Friday. On Saturday it is open in the morning from 08.15 to 12.30 hours. It is open 24 hours for telephones, (see **Telephones**). Other post offices are open from 08.15 to 13.30 hours, and 08.15 to 12.30 hours on Saturday. Stamps can be bought not only at post offices but also at tobacconists (*tabacchi*).

Rates are currently as follows: postcards 650 *lire*, letters within the EC 750 *lire*, outside the EC 850 *lire*; special delivery and express 3,000 *lire* (plus postage). The post within Italy and into Italy is notoriously slow (often more than a week) but even ordinary post is much quicker going out of the country.

Public Holidays

Shops, offices, schools and most museums are closed on the following days, which are national holidays:

1 January
6 January (Epiphany)
Easter Monday
25 April (Liberation Day, 1945)
1 May (Labour Day)
1st Sunday in June (Proclamation of the Republic)
15 August (Assumption of the Virgin)
1 November (All Saints)
8 December (Immaculate Conception)

25 and 26 December
Note that the state museums in
Florence and Tuscany are closed
on these days, except 6 January,
15 August, 1 November,
8 December and 26 December.
They are also closed on 1st
Sunday of June. **All Florence is
closed on its feast day, 24 June**.

Public Transport

Inside Florence you can walk to
just about anywhere in the
compact centre, but for an
expedition, say, to the church of
San Miniato, you may want to
take a bus or taxi.

Taxis

Taxis can be hailed, though you
will be lucky to find one passing
when you want one. Otherwise
find a taxi rank (an obvious one is
the station; but they are fairly
frequent) or call a radio taxi
telephone number such as
(055) 4390 or (055) 4798.

*An ATAF bus running along the
Arno towards the Ponte Vecchio*

Buses

The bus service in any foreign
city can be daunting but people
are generally helpful. Almost all
the routes in Florence that you
are likely to want pass by the
station, and there you can
enquire of an official which and
where to board. The service is
reasonably frequent; of course
the vehicles can get very
crowded in the rush-hours. You
should obtain a ticket (and
preferably also your return)
from a *tabaccaio* shop or a bar
with a bus-ticket (ATAF) sticker,
and stamp it on entry at the rear
of the bus. You can now travel on
as many buses as you like for 60
minutes (with a 1,200 lira ticket)
or 120 minutes (with a 1,500 lira
ticket).
Exit is from the centre of the bus,
and it is advisable to position
yourself beforehand, as the
Italians do. Drivers are
invariably obliging if you ask
them to tell you when to get off.
No 7 goes to Fiésole; no 13 goes
to Piazzale Michelangelo and
San Miniato; no 17b goes to the
Villa Camerata campsite and
youth hostel off Viale Righi.
To destinations outside Florence,
there is a choice between the
bus and the train. Unfortunately
getting the bus can be
complicated. Different bus
companies run to different
locations from different places.
But here are the departure
points (all of them close to the
railway station) and telephone
information numbers of the main
ones with a note of where they
go:
CAP, Largo Fratelli Alinari 9/10
(tel: 214637) for Impruneta,
Prato;

COPIT, Largo Fratelli Alinari 9/10 (tel: 214637) for Abetone, Cutigliano, Pistóia, Poggio a Caiano;
LAZZI, Piazza Stazione 4–6r (tel: 215154) for Bagni di Lucca, Empoli, Forte dei Marmi (for Carrara), Livorno, Lucca,

Duomo and Giotto's Campanile

Montecatini Terme, Pisa, Pistóia, Prato, Viaréggio;
SITA, Via Santa Caterina da Siena 15r (tel: 483651; 211487 Saturday and Sunday) for Arezzo, Bibbiena, Certaldo,

Empoli, Poggibonsi, San
Gimignano, Siena, Volterra.
These are direct; for some
places you will have to change.

Trains

The train is more comfortable
than a bus but generally less
frequent, especially if you want to
go to some of the smaller places.
However, it may be quicker if
there is a direct line. It is, for
instance, easier and quicker to
take the train from Florence to
Pisa (one goes on the hour every
hour) but to go to Siena (to which
there is no direct line) it is easier
and quicker to take the SITA
rapido bus which goes about
every half hour on the motorway.
Places to which there is a good
service from the station at Santa
Maria Novella include Pisa,
Arezzo, Lucca and Viaréggio. At
the station, seek the rail
information office, which is on the
right as you arrive.

Senior Citizens

Senior citizens (over 60) of the
EC, and of a number of other
countries with which Italy has a
reciprocal agreement (not
including the US), may enter
communal and state museums
free, on production of their
passport. Check with the tourist
office for any other concessions.

Students and Youths

Up to the age of 26 you may
qualify for a cheaper
'Transalpino' rail-ticket for
reaching and travelling in Italy,
and there are student discounts
on air-fares (enquire at student
travel agencies).
See **Accommodation** for youth
hostels and campsites in
Florence or contact:

Associazione Italiana Alberghi
per la Gioventu, Via Cavour 44,
Rome (tel: (06) 4871152).
There is a 'sleeping-bag hostel'
at the Villa Favard, Via Rocca
Tedalda, from June to
September, and two youth
hostels; Villa Camerata, Viale
Righi 2–4 (tel: 601451); Santa
Monaca, Via Santa Monaca 6 (tel:
268338).
Under 18s may enter museums
free under the same terms as
Senior citizens.

Telephones

The dialling tone on Italian
telephones is a sharp unbroken
hum.
A series of very rapid pips
means you are being connected.
A ringing telephone gives a
series of long beeps, and an
engaged signal is more rapid.
Italians say *pronto* ('ready')
when they pick up the
telephone. Visitors can be
connected with an operator in
their own country (in order to
reverse charges etc) by dialing
172 followed by the national
code.

International calls:

Italy's international code is 39.
Then follows the city or district
code: for Florence 055 (but
callers who are dialling Florence
from abroad should remove the
initial 0, thus 010 39 55).
Last comes the personal number,
which in Florence may be 4, 6 or
7 digits.
When you are dialling out of the
country, 00 gets you an
international line.
Britain's international code is 44,
thus 00 44
United States is 1, thus 00 1
Australia 00 61

DIRECTORY

It's clearly an SIP phone box (the Italian telephone service)!

Eire 00 353.
Then remove the initial nought of the area code and to that add the personal number.

For more difficult international calls, use a hotel or a SIP office (SIP is the Italian telephone service). In Florence there is one open 24 hours in the Central Post Office in Via Pellicceria; another is open from 07.30 to 21.30 hours, in the station. Hotels are entitled to charge a commission on telephone calls, and they certainly do!

Otherwise, almost every bar in Italy has a telephone, and there are many in public places. They take 100 and 200 *lire* coins, tokens or *gettoni*, and in many cases now phonecards, which can be bought from *tabacchi* (tobacco shops) in 5,000 or 10,000 *lire* denominations. (You must tear off the corner before you can use them.)

A local call is charged flat rate; otherwise there are banded costings, cheapest in the evening and most expensive in the morning.

Time

Italy keeps the same time as the rest of Europe except for Britain; which is one hour earlier virtually all year except for about three weeks in October, when it has the same time. New York and Montreal are six hours earlier and Sydney eight hours later in summer.

Tipping

Tipping in Italy is truly up to you. If you do not tip no one will make a fuss or say anything, let alone start shouting. A service charge is very often already added to the bill in a restaurant, but if it is not, there is no obligation or even expectation that you should add one. However, if you wish to tip decently, it will be welcomed and appreciated. An extra 1,000 *lire* or so a head is acceptable for exceptional service and 500 *lire* is the minimum that should be given for any service.

Toilets

Public conveniences are not Italy's strong point: they are very rare. However, they do exist in stations, and of course every bar has one, and there are lots of bars. However, the toilet in a bar is private and it is important to ask to use it and to expect to pay for it, even if it is only by buying a coffee you didn't want. Because too many tourists have come in just to use the toilet, bar-owners have often resorted to hanging the sign *guasto* (broken) on the toilet door. This is seldom true, though it tends to indicate a rather shabby example. Toilets are often marked *signori* (men) and *signore* (women).

Tourist Offices

Florence and the cities of
Tuscany take their tourism
seriously, so their tourist offices
stay open, speak English, are
helpful and have lots of
information. The only problem is
that they are very 'patriotic', so it
is almost impossible to find out
about one city or area when you
are in another. Ask in Florence
about Siena and they may as well
not have heard of the place,
though they will tell you all about
small villages in the
administrative province of
Florence.
In **Florence**: the main office is at
Via Cavour 1R (tel: 290832/3),
there is another at the station (in
Piazza Stazione tel: 212245; turn
left as you arrive) and one close
by the Palazzo Vecchio, behind
one wing of the Uffizi (Chiasso
Baroncelli 17 and 19r, tel:
2302124). These are open from
08.30 to 18.30 hours in summer,
09.00 to 15.00 hours in winter.
There is another also at Fiésole
(Piazza Mino 37, tel: 598822).
In **Arezzo**: Piazza Risorgimento
116 (tel: (0575) 20839/23952).

*The boys in blue: some local police
in Pisa*

In **Lucca**: Piazza Guidiccioni 2
(tel: (0583) 491205).
In **Pisa**: Piazza Duomo (tel: (050)
560464) or at the station (tel:
(050) 42291).
In **Pistóia**: Via Gramsci 110 (tel:
(0573) 34326).
In **Prato**: Via Muzzi 51 (tel: (0574)
35141).
In **San Gimignano**: Piazza
Duomo (tel: (0577) 940008).
In **Siena**: Piazza del Campo 56
(tel: (0577) 280551).
Expect to catch these for certain
only in the morning, but in
summer they should be open
from 15.30 to 19.00 hours as
well.

Travel Agencies

If you want a guided tour of
Florence try 'Ufficio Guide
Turistiche Cooperative Giotto',
Viale Gramsci 9a (tel: 2478188).
Otherwise any travel agent will
offer bus tours of the city or
excursions to other places in
Tuscany. For rail tickets it is best
to try CIT or Wagon Lits or of
course the station; not all do
them. There are several airline
offices in Florence: look them up
under *Linee Aeree*. There is an
information line about travel
agencies: FIAVET, tel: (055)
294900.

LANGUAGE

If you have no Italian at all, the most important thing to concentrate on is getting the names of people and places right. Many Italians can speak English, but no one will understand if you mispronounce or mumble the place where you want to go or the person you want to see. Pronunciation is simple, once you know the rules about 'hard' and 'soft' *c*, *sc*, and *g*, and so long as you speak clearly, opening the mouth wide, using tongue and teeth.

Pronunciation

C is soft before *i* or *e* (= English *ch* or *sh*) – this *sh* or softer *c* is a Florentine dialect change. *C* before *a*, *o* or *u* is hard, and also if followed by an *h*. Thus *ciao* (goodbye or hello) is soft, *chiacchierare* (to chatter) is hard. However, less educated Tuscans often aspirate hard *c* to a heavy *h*: *casa* becomes 'hasa'. *Sc* is soft (= English *sh*) before *i* or *e*, hard if followed by an *h*. The same goes for *g*: *gi* is soft (= English *j*), *ga* and *ghi* are hard (= English hard *g*, eg garden). Italian accents indicate stress, and it can be important to get that right. *Caffè* (coffee) has the stress on the last syllable, which is unusual and is indicated by the accent. But the stress is often not on the last syllable but one, but on the last but two, for example both the Medici family and *medici*, doctors, are pronounced 'mèdici' and not medìci, as we would expect in English.

Vocabulary

It is a good idea to use words of common politeness, even if you have to speak English for what you really want:

please per piacère, per favòre, per cortesìa
thank you gràzie
not at all! prego
good morning buon giorno
good evening buona sera
good night buona notte
goodbye arriverderla, arriverderci, buona sera **in the evening**, ciao (**to children or the young or friends – or in response to ciao**)
hello ciao
   (**on the telephone**) pronto
I beg your pardon scusi
that's all right va bene
excuse me permesso
can I help you? posso aiutarla?
I'm sorry mi dispiace

It is usual to address men as *Signore* and women as *Signora* and girls – whatever exactly that may mean – as *Signorina*.

Basic Vocabulary

yes sì
no no
today oggi
tomorrow domani
morning mattina
afternoon pomeriggio
evening sera
night notte
day giorno
week settimana
month mese
year anno
hour ora
early presto, di buon'ora
late tardi, in ritardo
large grande
small piccolo, -a
hot caldo, -a
cold freddo, -a
good buono, -a
bad cattivo, -a
where is? dov'è?

straight ahead diritto, sempre diritto
left a sinistra
right a destra
how much? quanto?
open aperto
closed chiuso
working day feriale
holiday festivo
slowly lentamente
entrance entrata
exit uscita
all tutto
many/much molto
why? perchè?
when? quando?
what? cosa?
upstairs sopra
downstairs in basso
inside dentro
expensive caro
cheap economico
come in! avanti!

Phrases

I do not understand non capisco
do you speak English? parla Inglese?
I cannot speak Italian non parlo Italiano
please speak slowly parli adagio, la prego
what do you want? cosa desidera?
what is the matter? cosa c'è?
where are we going? dove andiamo?
I shall stay here resterò qui
is there a doctor near by? c'è un médico qui vicino?
call a policeman at once chiami subito un vigile
I am feeling very ill mi sento molto male

At the Hotel

a twin-bedded room una camera a due letti
a double room una camera matrimonale
a child's bed letto da bambino
a cot una culla
can you give me a room for the night? mi può dare una camera per la notte?
what is the price of a room for each day? quanto costa al giorno una camera?
I do not like this room non mi piace questa camera
have you no cheaper room? non ne ha una che costa meno?

In the Restaurant

can we have lunch here? si può fare mangiare qui?
have you a table for...? avete un tavola per...?
we do not want a full meal non desideriamo un pasto completo
may we have another table? potremmo spostarci?
where is the washroom? dov'è la toiletta?
please may I have the menu? ci dia la carta, per piacere?
the bill, please il conto, per favore

At the Garage

fill it up, please faccia il pieno, per favore
I would like ... litres of petrol vorrei... litri di benzina
My car won't go La macchina non funziona
brakes freni
flat tyre gomma forata
fan belt cinghia del ventilatore
water acqua
oil olio
lights luci
windscreen parabrezza

Food

lamb agnello
hors d'oeuvres antipasto

LANGUAGE

roast meat arrosto
boiled meats bollito misto
game cacciagione
meat carne
rabbit coniglio
cauliflower cavolfiore
cabbage cavolo
onion cipolle
raw crudo
sweets dolci
liver fegato
flat pasta fettuccine
pork maiale
beef manzo, bistecca
figs fichi
cheese formaggio
omelette frittata, omelette
fried fritto
fruit frutta
shellfish frutti di mare
mushrooms funghi
prawns gamberi
ice-cream gelato
grilled griglia (alla)
salad insalata
lemon limone
fruit salad macedonia
jam marmellata
apple mela
honey miele
soup minestra
nuts noci
veal knuckle osso buco
oysters ostriche
bread roll panino
cream panna
potatoes patate
pear pera
peach pesca
fish pesce
peas piselli
chicken pollo
tomato pomodoro
grapefruit pompelmo
ham prosciutto
plums prugne, susine
rice riso
sausage salsiccia
sardines sarde

escalopes scaloppine
sole sogliola
spinach spinaci
sugar zucchero
sandwich tramezzino
eggs uova
grapes uva
green vegetables verdure
veal vitello
courgettes zucchini
soup zuppa

Drink
mineral water acqua minerale
beer birra
fruit juice succo di frutta
milk latte
coffee caffè
black coffee espresso
tea tè
chocolate cioccolato
glass bicchiere
bottle bottiglia
half-bottle mezza bottiglia
dry secco
sweet dolce

Transport
airport aeroporto
bus autobus
seaport porto
motorboat motoscafo
train treno
ticket biglietto
single andata
return andata e ritorno
first/second class
prima/seconda classe
station stazione
sleeping berth cuccetta

Shops
bank banca
bookshop libreria
butcher macelleria
chemist farmacia
cleaner tintoria
fishmonger pescheria
greengrocer fruttivendolo

grocer alimentare, pizzicheria
hairdresser parrucchiere, -a
market mercato
optician ottico
post office ufficio postale
stationer cartoleria
tobacconists tabacchi
tourist bureau officio di turismo
travel agent agenzia di viaggio

Numbers

one uno, una
two due
three tre
four quattro
five cinque
six sei
seven sette
eight otto
nine nove
ten dieci
fifty cinquanta
one hundred cento
one thousand mille

Days of the Week

Sunday domenica
Monday lunedì
Tuesday martedì
Wednesday mercoledì
Thursday giovedì
Friday venerdì
Saturday sabato

Months of the Year

January gennaio
February febbraio
March marzo
April aprile
May maggio
June giugno
July luglio
August agosto
September settembre
October ottobre
November novembre
December dicembre

Glossary of Art & Architectural Terms

architrave horizontal frame above a door
badia abbey
campanile bell tower (often free standing)
camposanto cemetery
certosa charterhouse
chiaroscuro distribution of light and shade in painting
cupola dome
diptych painting which is in two sections
duomo cathedral
faience decorated earthenware and porcelain
grisaille shades of grey
hypogeum underground burial chamber of Etruscans
intarsia wood, marble or metal inlay
loggia open-sided gallery or arcade
lunette semi-circular space on ceiling or over door decorated with painting or relief
maestà Madonna and Child in glory
mandorla almond shape of light around figure in religious art
pala large altar-piece
pietà painting or sculpture of Virgin and dead Christ
polyptych work of art with four or more panels
putto nude sculpture or painting of cherubic child
sinopia preliminary sketch (on wall) for fresco
tempera egg based paint popular before oils came in (in the Renaissance)
tessera small cubes used in mosaic work
tondo round painting or relief
trecento the 14th century
quattrocento the 15th century
cinquecento the 16th century

INDEX/ACKNOWLEDGEMENTS

The Automobile Association would like to thank the following photographers, libraries, associations and individuals for their assistance in the preparation of this book.

BARRIE SMITH took all the photographs in this book (© AA Photo Library) except:

AA PHOTO LIBRARY 67 Pisa, 74/5 Siena Duomo, 76 Palazzo Pubblico and Campo Siena, 79 Tuscany view, 96/7 Leather goods, 102 Siena Campo, 104 Ponte Vecchio.

P HOLBERTON 20 Giovanni de Paolo.

INTERNATIONAL PHOTOBANK 6 Ponte Vecchio, 13 Statue of Neptune.

MARY EVANS PICTURE LIBRARY 7 Dante Alighieri, 11 Cosimo I de Medici, 12 Giovanni de Medici, 17

Filippo Brunelleschi, 18 Luca della Robbia, 31 Lorenzo de Medici, 46 Fra Angelico.

NATURE PHOTOGRAPHERS LTD 80 Bee-eater (P R Sterry), 82/3 Olives, 84 Great reed warbler (K J Carlson), 85 Crested porcupine (S C Bisserott).

SPECTRUM COLOUR LIBRARY Cover Duomo & skyline, 16 Painting of S Maria Novella, 61 Arezzo, 64 Pienza, 69 Prato Cathedral, 105 Palazzo della Logge, 115 Della Francesca frescos.

WORLD PICTURES 24 Florence, 94 Duomo, 112 Carriage, 118 Duomo & Giotto's Campanile.

Thanks also to **Robert Kane** for his revision work, and to the **Automobile Club d'Italia** for their assistance in updating the Directory section.

Copy editor for original edition: Jo Sturges
For this revision: Copy editor Jenny Fry; verifier P Leahy